Create Your Dream Art- Business

BE A SM-ART-PRENEUR

Rashmi Suthar

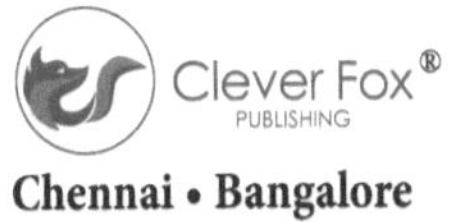

Chennai • Bangalore

CLEVER FOX PUBLISHING
Chennai, India

Published by CLEVER FOX PUBLISHING 2023
Copyright © Rashmi Suthar 2023

All Rights Reserved.
ISBN: 978-93-56487-62-8

for
SHIVA
the God inside all of us

Chapters

Hello there! I am Rashmi Suthar. How are you doing today? I had a dream. It was a beautiful one. In that dream, I was abundant in terms of health, wealth, and peace. I was in my studio, which overlooked the mountains. I opened the windows and looked out. The sky was beautiful, and the air smelled fresh. I had all the art materials that I needed in the studio, tubes of paint, paint brushes, easels, canvas, and all. And I met my group of mentees. I took them on a hike. It is a good day for a hike, don't you think? Come join me.

As artists, we are all good at imagination. So now I would like you to imagine that we are going on a hike together. It can be your favourite place, anywhere in the world. But to get to the hiking spot, we have to travel a bit by road. So grab your bags. I hope you have packed all your hiking gear. Oh, and do bring a book and a pen along to take notes, and load them onto the Jeep. Now you can hop on and wear your seat belts. There will be a few ups and downs along the way. But don't worry, I've got you!

Are you ready? As we travel to the hiking spot, I will tell you a bit about myself and how I, an architect, went on to become an artist and then an art business coach. And slowly, I will also share with you all the lessons I learned from my experiences in the last decade. With this, we will also work on establishing your dream art business. I am excited to travel this journey with you. Lets goo!

Prologue

From the beginning of my childhood, I was always a kid who loved to be alone. I spent a lot of time engrossed in thought and my imaginative world. Throughout my youth, I experienced intense emotions, often feeling unloved and unaccepted by my parents. Despite craving their attention, it never seemed enough.

One film that inspired me as a child was August Rush. It led me to believe that everyone is uniquely talented, with the universe working tirelessly to reveal those gifts. As I grew up, I aspired to join the Air Force. However, in 2016, I learned that the Indian Air Force did not accept women, leaving me disappointed with the system.

I possessed a natural creativity throughout my childhood, always enjoying drawing and painting. There was a TV show called "Sanju Ka Magic Pencil" that I adored; it featured a character who had a magic pencil capable of bringing anything he drew to life. This series spoke to my desire for self-expression and reinforced an underlying wish to pursue art.

Unfortunately, due to societal pressures and expectations from my parents, pursuing a career as an artist seemed impossible at the time; becoming an engineer or doctor was deemed the best choice.

I was fairly good at studying, so in class 12, I considered either pursuing aeronautical engineering or architecture. My cousin was already studying architecture, which made it an appealing choice. My parents expected me to be a top student to get into a prestigious college. Although there was immense pressure, I knew I was excellent and aimed for the best. Eventually, I got into the MSU College of Architecture, one of the top three in Gujarat.

Coming from a diverse school that celebrated various cultural festivals, transitioning to a more regional college was challenging. At first, I felt superior because of my background. However, I soon realised that everyone at MSU was uniquely talented and creative. The first seven months were difficult as I adjusted to living in the girls' hostel and sharing a room with regional students speaking different languages.

One of my early artistic inspirations came from one of my professors, Mayur Gupta. He was a rebel in the world of fine arts and stood out from the other professors. He allowed us to be ourselves and express our individuality, even smoking with a rebellious flair. Over the course of five years, he became one of my favourite professors, sparking my interest in sculpture and contemporary art. His work became an inspiration for me, shaping my abilities and pushing me to think outside the box in my architectural projects. I want to share a story about the first failure I experienced in my life. It shook me to my core after excelling in everything. It forced me to make peace with who I am and became the trigger for my personal journey to discover my true self beyond achievements, labels, and knowledge. I will talk more about my identity crisis later, but first, let me share this initial failure.

My teachers believed I was too smart for the programme and accused me of skipping classes. I ended up failing, and they recommended that I repeat the year. This came as a shock to me since I had performed well in my exams. In fact, I was even tutoring and helping my classmates who struggled with English. This setback at my college was devastating. I was working in Pune at my first internship, adjusting to a new city, and then receiving the news that I had failed. At that moment, I felt lost and broken, without any support.

Thankfully, my boss at the internship saw potential in me and offered me another year to work there. This gave me reassurance that I was capable. However, I couldn't help but feel frustrated with a society and world that couldn't accept an exceptional individual like myself.

I was in Pune, working at my first internship, when I first experienced the real world as an architect. This transition was significant because I was a young adult moving from my parents' home to college and then to a new city. When I heard that I had failed, there was no one around to support me. I was shocked and broken, feeling terrible for the first four hours. At a loss, I confided in my boss, who encouraged me to stay for another year, complimenting my work. Although I didn't doubt my abilities, society's expectations frustrated me.

In the next three hours, I realised that I possessed incredible resilience. Despite this setback, I chose to focus on what could still be accomplished. Determined to prove myself, I decided to pursue a photography internship. As I walked towards a renowned photographer's studio nearby, tears streamed down my face. With courage, I told him about my situation and my desire to become a photographer. He advised me to process my feelings overnight before returning.

After much reflection and emotional turmoil, I found the strength to rise above disappointment and passionately pursue my goals without anyone's help: a quality every artist should have for success and resilience in the face of adversity. When life gives you lemons, you make lemonade.

When life gives you
lemons, make a
lemonade

Professionally I was working as an architect, and after that failure, I continued to work for the same firm. I decided not to join the photographer at the last moment. Wanting to pursue photography was a very impulsive decision I had made, so I continued to be an architect. It was during this time that I also developed an "imposter syndrome" that made me constantly question myself on whether I was really good enough or a loser. In fact, it took me an entire year to digest the fact that I had failed and had to restart as an architect.

Every so often, life gives us opportunities to pause, reflect, and rework on ourselves. It was at this very moment that my life decided to give me that pause in the form of a break from my education. It gave me that much-needed exposure to what real life was. I had an entire year to think about what was happening in my life.

One of the most significant shifts in my life was learning to depend on and love someone. That someone had always been present in my life, but I had never fully

He came to me, all the way from Ahmedabad to Pune, just to be there for me when I was upset. At that point, I was in a vulnerable state, in need of companionship. This was my first encounter with love, and I was very grateful to have someone by my side, supporting me through my failures.

That was when I realised that love is bigger than anything in life, and I chose to pursue it irrespective of what happened. Motivated by this newfound support, I took a leap of faith and decided to take our relationship more seriously. As a young adult, I was heavily swayed by my emotions, which led me to make a rather bold decision. I chose to move to his city, leaving behind a stable job.

In his city, I found another job. Despite him being a junior and not in a position to provide financial support, I was determined to make it work. The harsh realities of life hit me hard in 2013. I was young and lost, unsure of my path. I had always been an achiever, consistently performing well, so this failure was a massive blow to my family. My mother, although supportive, was equally concerned. She provided emotional support. My father, It was now on me to become financially independent. I was still a student, and I found myself navigating a new reality where money was not only important but had to be independently earned. I had to balance my studies with the necessity of sustaining myself.

All this while, the relationship, despite being supportive and nurturing, was also marked by our youthful naivety.

We were both young, love-struck, and without a clear plan for our futures. My boyfriend, being a local, had a roof over his head and support from his parents. Yet, we were both caught up in the whirlwind of our love, neglecting our education and not making any significant progress in our lives. It was at this time that I also started networking professionally. For the first time, I was connecting with interior designers and architects to kick-start my career. Using the skills I had acquired as a student, I managed to secure an exciting project. One of my talents has always been my vivid imagination and ability to sketch.. It came naturally to me. The artist in me began this new chapter, I found that the artist in me was coming alive, and I was ready to embrace it.

This proved to be a tremendous advantage in my life, allowing me to design concepts that people were willing to pay for. Even at a young age, people were drawn to my ideas. Usually, people use youngsters for their skills and not their ideas, but here I had people trusting me for my ideas and were willing to pay me for my concepts. Looking back, I realise that this was the beginning of a journey where people trusted and valued my unique concepts, colour schemes, and aesthetics.

I found myself immersed in creating new concepts for bedrooms and living rooms, and getting paid for these sketches was exciting. I loved that job. Alongside this, I was also given the opportunity to accompany a commercial interior designer to observe the execution of these designs in reality. That year was filled with invaluable exposure, allowing me to truly understand the professional world of architecture and interior design.

While I did secure a job at a large company after my stint in Pune, I soon realised a traditional job was not for me. The corporate environment did not suit me, and the work was not fulfilling. I was tasked with drafting AutoCAD drawings, which involved sitting at a computer and designing things that were not even my own ideas. So, I decided to freelance. I found out that I loved free-lancing.

One of my clients, Nikhil, an interior designer from Ahmedabad, recognised my talent and offered me the kind of opportunity I had been seeking. This relationship proved to be fruitful, as he later became one of my art patrons. Nikhil saw the artist in me way before I fully realised it myself.

During this year of professional growth and exploration, my personal life took a tumultuous turn. My boyfriend and his parents realised that his academics were suffering due to our relationship. As I got to know him better, I discovered he was involved in some unhealthy habits, which negatively impacted his life and those around him. Despite attempts to help him, he decided to move to Germany. This was the second time that year that I was shattered. However, I also did start seeing that some of his ways of life were not aligning with what I wanted in a relationship, leading to the end of our relationship.

This was my first heartbreak, a painful experience after all the drastic steps I had taken for love — moving cities, and changing jobs. In one year, I had gone from feeling like a failure to dealing with my first heartbreak. It was a year of significant upheaval, but it also brought with it valuable lessons about life and love.

For anyone reading this story who has experienced heartbreak, I want you to know that you should be grateful for this first love in your life. You may not realise it but it is these heartbreaks that help you stand on your feet and become the strong person you are today. It is during these times that you learn to balance your emotions with reality.

That year for me was a whirlwind of experiences – failures, heartbreaks, the harsh reality of financial independence, and conditional parental love as well. Of course, I will not say that my father's attitude remained unchanged; he resumed his support after a while, but the entire episode had significantly altered my perspective. Most parents in India put a lot of pressure on their kids to succeed, and without it, the kids are not given the same kind of love. It made me question the nature of parental love—is it truly unconditional, or is it subject to a child's success?

As the year came to an end, I found myself alone again, with no support. But it was also a time for introspection. As a child, it was always when I was alone that I found my peace, and this time again, I was alone. I was finally ready to face my parents and decided to move back in with them. Having had enough time to recover from what had happened, they welcomed me with open arms.

They asked me about my plans, but I was at a loss. My mother suggested I return to school and complete my degree. I expressed to them that, having seen real life, a degree did not feel very important. My father, holding onto his middle-class beliefs, emphasised the importance of a degree. Despite my initial resistance, I decided to go back to school.

I had to face another set of emotions. I was always an assertive person, and my juniors had always shown me respect, sometimes out of fear due to the hierarchy that existed in our college. Now, I had to sit with them on the same bench, which was initially embarrassing. One junior, Dhara, who eventually became my friend, was the first one to smile back at me. With time, I adjusted and made new friends.

I was in my final year, having already completed an internship. The year I failed was supposed to be an internship year anyway, so instead of just six months of work experience, I had a year and a half, which was an amazing advantage. This significantly enhanced my portfolio. The lessons I learned from my failures and the experiences with love, relationships, networking, and business relationships all enriched my life in ways I could not have imagined.

So, I would like to say thank you to all my failures. At the moment, failures might have seemed like the end of the world, but when you look back with a bird's-eye view, you realise that they were just stepping stones, adding to your life's portfolio and teaching you invaluable lessons. Those heartbreaks and failures are often just a planned strategy for your growth.

That year was very eventful and filled with lessons that made me richer in experience. It was also the year I got to work on a celebrity's farmhouse. I was working with celebrities during that period. I was in Pune, working with them at a wonderful contemporary firm.

The chief architect was a graduate from London, and being coached by him was an amazing opportunity I got.. And then there was the whole experience I gained from Nikhil as a freelancer, so all of these experiences were piling up from my skills in graphic design, 3D design, sketching, networking, and selling. This added to my portfolio for a year and a half. All this happened before I graduated, so I went back to school as an actual senior. I had a very good perspective on what I was doing.

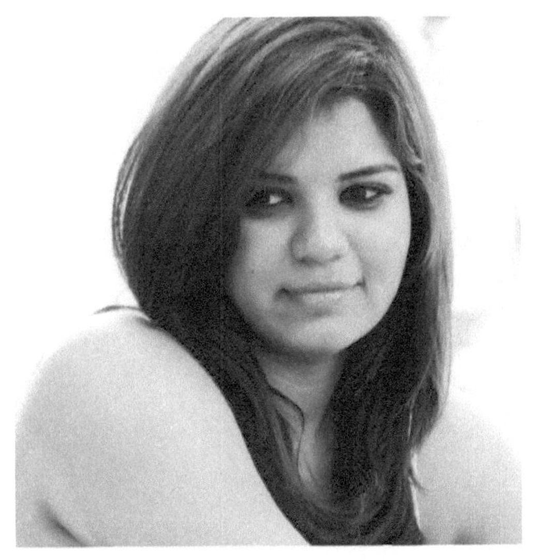

Me, as a student of Architecture

Gokarna

In Architecture, the fifth year is the final year, and it was the best year for me. Why? First, because it was the last year. And second, it gave me the freedom to choose a subject and a topic that I wanted to design. In the preceding years, we were handed spaces that we had to design, like urban spaces, houses, landscapes, and hospitality. So finally, we had the opportunity to put it all in one space of our choice. For our thesis, we had the freedom to choose what, where, and how we were going to design.

The best thing we got to do was travel. You can get out of your house and be paid for it. It was at this juncture that I met Santosh, a friend of mine and a very important person in my journey as an artist, because he saw me as an artist and empowered me as an artist way before I knew I was an artist. I met him in my last year, and I wrote my first book, which is not published but is in the University Library. The Science of Spirituality is based on the research I did for my thesis, and it is a very important part of my life. Santosh is a corporate dude working for a large multinational company. He saw that I was talented and helped me through my thesis. We had to find a site as the base for our project. He is a travel freak.

He said,'*Why do you want to pick a site in Gujrat? Why don't you do something interesting?*"

Knowing that my topic was spirituality and science, he suggested we go to a beautiful town in Karnataka called Gokarna.

'*Let's have a vacation, and in turn, you can do your research*', he said.

I was sold out. I loved this idea, and I researched a little about Gokarna. It had a very strong spiritual angle, and the landscape had both the mountains and the beach. That was a perfect site. It is where I wanted to execute and design an ashram.

For me, an ashram was a place that accommodated all age groups. That is what Ashram means in Sanskrit. It is one of the four stages of life.
- Childhood
- Teenagehood
- Married life and
- Retirement

This is what an ashram is in India. Architecturally, I

thought that it was just a space. But then, when I got to know the meaning of it, I felt like I wanted to serve everyone. And that is when I decided I was going to serve everyone and create a community space that is called an ashram.

As I write this, I am connecting the dots, and I realise that, in a way, the community that I am creating aligns with the vision I had for my thesis. Now the vision for me is to bring all these age groups together in a community where all of us can support and love each other. It is called The Dream 100. I have unconsciously been realising that dream of mine—that first quest for spirituality and science. When I picture my dream community, a space that caters to all age groups, with foundations built on love, honesty, integrity, and support for each other, it is all about living alongside people who have that warrior spirit but also stay genuinely themselves.

They are all about giving back and making things better for everyone around them. So, I took this trip to Gokarna with my buddy, who was of such huge help on this project. We were digging into how those incredible Indian temples were put together, each spot radiating this amazing energy and togetherness.

Seeing how those tight-knit villages in India rally around a sick kid made me realise the stark contrast to city life. In cities, your neighbour might not even peek out when you are unwell. After soaking up all that insight from speaking to the locals in the village, I stumbled upon this massive eight-acre site. That is when it hit me—I am going to create something special here, and that will be The Ashram, a place filled with spirituality and all about bringing people together.

This project became my absolute favourite in architecture; it is where I found my identity. Now, I began to see myself more as a thought leader than just someone putting up buildings in any industry. I had become passionate about how things should be in our everyday human settings.

When I brought this vision back to school, pro architects really dug it, and that fueled my research even more. Stage two was all about proving this concept through a case study because, well, nobody in India had thought about this kind of Ashram before. There was not anything to point to and say, 'Look, it exists!' Unlike most spiritual spaces built around a guru, my Ashram is not about a single face. It is all about philosophy, principles of love, honesty, trust, and, yeah, a bit of science too! I wanted to make something that makes logical sense rather than just being all spiritual vibes. It is more of a scientific commune, you see? I am out here trying to show that this concept can actually work.

Rishikesh

That phase was tough, I'll tell you. Most architects are pros at hospitals, museums, buildings—you name it. But designing an Ashram? That was a whole new ball game, something no one had a clue about. I had to justify something that didn't have a playbook. So, I embarked on this journey—next stop: Rishikesh!

That place was something else! The quest was not just about designing a spiritual space but digging deep into my own inner journey. I had all these questions swirling inside me, from why my mother is so spiritual while my father is all about science to why studying science sometimes feels like it leads nowhere. I was on a quest for answers, seeking that divine presence. Rishikesh, by the Ganges, blew my mind! The energy there was just incredible. I did the whole plunge into the Ganga—crazy, right? But it felt like tapping into something truly special.

I remember that crazy day vividly—January 1st, 2015, I

woke up thinking, 'New year, new me, right?' So, I decided to go for it, to wash away my sins with a holy bath. It was more like an 'Into the Wild' kind of adventure I wanted to experience. I asked my buddy if he was up for it, just to test our mettle. Jumping into that water... oh boy, it was freezing! I mean, we are talking glacier-level coldness! The Ganges was no joke that day, rushing like crazy. I went in and felt those chills pierce through me. I swear, even talking about it gives me shivers!

I barely lasted a few seconds—just in there, holding onto a rock for dear life. I dipped my head into that speedy water for like, what, maybe 20 seconds? Thought I was going to freeze solid right then and there. But when I emerged out onto this stunning white sandy beach in Rishikesh and closed my eyes, Whoa! That moment felt like my first encounter with something divine.

Picture this: I close my eyes, the sunlight hits me, and it is like a whole new beginning—a rebirth. I visualised something like Buddha slowly moving closer and closer until it merged into me, taking the shape of an infinity symbol.

Mind-blowing, right? I was so moved by that moment that I got it tattooed. The symbol of infinity. For me, it is not just a symbol; it is a reminder of that incredible experience.

So, my big takeaway from that whole journey? It is that fire to manifest this dream community. I am totally into making that happen, and things are falling into place step by step.

The concept of infinity and its interpretation within the philosophy of infinity are truly captivating. As a self-proclaimed geek and a passionate researcher, I am always seeking scientific evidence to support my beliefs and actions. This quest led me to the Bhagavad Gita, where I stumbled upon a fascinating perspective on infinity.

"Knowledge of goodness is seeing everything as one or infinity.'

The text suggests that a truly enlightened individual perceives everything as a singular entity or infinity. This revelation struck a chord with me, as I felt that my lifelong pursuit of knowledge closely mirrored this concept.

It hit me hard because, in life, we are constantly learning, right? And being 'good' is not just about others; it is about this energy, this effort to grow within ourselves. The Gita talks about working on yourself, becoming better, and that journey ultimately leading to goodness. In it, Krishna talks about this connection to the divine, seeing everyone and everything as one. That is when I decided to immortalise that concept with a tattoo of that shloka on my body. And yes, that is the infinity tattoo! It is that shloka written in the shape of the infinity symbol.

It was like my first 'Hey, God!' moment. I was so happy this journey took me to the serene landscapes of Rishikesh; that place is a goldmine! It is where I delved deep into the structures and the philosophy of ashrams —the whole mentor-mentee relationship, that deep-rooted respect and love for the Guru in our Indian tradition. I came to understand that that bond is one of the most sacred relationships one can have.

As a coach, I believe that the essence of goodness is not just about being righteous towards others; it lies in the relentless strive towards self-improvement and personal growth.

The teachings are more of a way of life than just a religion. I'm totally on board with that! The whole spirituality tied to Hinduism—I realised we are not about religion at all. It is the people who are causing all the fuss. The universe, or whatever you call it—I go with 'universe' as my higher power—is never meant for these divisions. Buddha had it right. The biggest trick in the world is making us feel separate.

As I dug deeper into Hinduism and Buddhism, I noticed the connection and how Buddhism sprang from Hinduism. I got intrigued by Buddha's teachings, and that is when these gurus started popping up in my life. I don't just have one Guru—I have a bunch! There is this book, 'One Life, Many Masters'—I have not read it yet, but the title hits home. I feel like it is me! In this life, I learn from everyone and everything. It is not just people;

it is the situations, the pain, and even the trees that have taught me lessons along the way. As I delved deeper into my research, two books—the Bhagavad Gita and the Ashtavakra Gita—completely transformed my life. I am urging you all to read the Ashtavakra Gita; it is a game-changer. Now, books and mentors; they find you, not the other way around. The Bhagavad Gita came into my life like an infinity symbol, revealing Krishna and Arjuna's incredible relationship and the life lessons applicable in today's world—leadership, business, and relationships. Everything is in there. Osho's interpretation simplified things, making Gita's wisdom more accessible.

In my research, I discovered the Guru-Shishya tradition's intricate transmission in Hinduism. Knowledge transmission was quite flawed. For example, this is what I think happened. Gurus teach under a tree, with students jotting down their respective interpretations in their respective styles. This led to multiple perceptions and, eventually, many different practices. The knowledge got tangled up in the process of being transferred, not at its source. Unfortunately, the distributors—let us call them 'knowledge distributors"—exploited and twisted it to maintain control, much like media manipulation today.

This manipulation of knowledge has led many to lose faith in Hinduism's true essence as a way of life. People often don't dive deep enough to grasp its value; they see it as blind rituals and traditions. Questioning these practices is where the real understanding begins.

Surprisingly, Hindu spirituality was always rooted in logic and science, not falsehoods. My visits to various ashrams revealed something extraordinary: their meticulous design. These spaces incorporated good sunlight, ventilation, and indigenous materials—creating structures that held positive energy, offering peace and tranquillity to all. As an architect, it just made perfect sense.

When You are Lost
you are Found

My next step involved bringing this concept to urban spaces, infusing the same tranquillity and emotional sharing found in ashrams. I am still deeply invested in this project because we are missing this in our modern lives. Designing spaces that reflect these philosophies for a global audience became my mission. Spaces matter profoundly—they evoke emotions much like art. A dark painting can make you feel dark; a vibrant one uplifts you. Emotions are deeply tied to our senses.

Buddhism became my next exploration. Buddha was the master of the senses. But this journey was no longer just a project; it became an internal quest—a search for my own identity and purpose. It is funny how getting lost in that quest helped me find myself. You know what they say: when you are lost, that is when you are truly found.

After Rishikesh, I was engulfed in questions about my existence—Who am I? Why did God say hi? What is this, God? Is it science? I was looking for answers, finding none in science, textbooks, or even the Gita. Seeking the essence of spirituality, I headed to *Kumbh Mela*, the largest event that happens in India that can even be visible from space, hoping to find answers amid a sea of spirituality. It was an individual quest, not just a project. While the thesis was secondary, my inner queries took over.

With each step, I found more complexities, especially at *Kumbh Mela*. Witnessing devoted saints meditating without food for years shocked and surprised me.

Amidst all this, I met a ninety-two-year-old refugee, a saint from Bangladesh, who patiently answered my questions. I questioned myths about Ganesha's elephant face and God's ethical dilemmas, finding them baseless.

Eventually, this saint suggested I read the *Ashtavakra Gita*. It became the beacon in my quest, providing answers and closing my chapter of self-discovery. Unlike the Bhagavad Gita, this one narrates Raja Janak's story—a king who found Sita, but no one knew who her birth parents were. Sita's father, Raja Janak, asks questions about knowledge, liberation, and passion from his mentor, Ashtavakra.

Ashtavakra, a liberated soul, advises Raja Janak to shun material desires and practice tolerance, sincerity, compassion, contentment, and truthfulness for spiritual liberation. As Raja Janak's questions resonated with mine, *Ashtavakra*'s wisdom answered my questions and enlightened me.

So, as I delved deeper into the *Ashtavakra* Gita, I realised that the crux of spirituality was within me, the common connection between science and spirituality. I discovered that the 'I' or ego attaches itself to the world, creating a false sense of importance. Surrendering this 'me' opened my eyes to a different perspective, a realisation that everyone's struggles and joys, regardless of how big or small, stem from the same core emotions.

Ashtavakra's wisdom unified me with myself, discussing the duality of life, impermanence, permanence, emotions, and more. It was my second revelation, acknowledging that I am the amalgamation of science and spirituality. This epiphany became the bedrock of my existence.

Returning to my thesis, I presented my final project for my final year. I was so very invested in it that I had actually made eight different models in various materials (somehow the number 8 is again infinity, and it seems to have followed me throughout my journey).

I tried to showcase the universal concept of the Ashram beyond religion. I presented it to a jury of five very experienced architects who appreciated my effort, and they told me that it was the most unique and exceptional work they had seen in all those years from any student in that college.

They encouraged me to not let this project end with the thesis but to continue it in my real life. It was sort of a turning point in my life.

We had two guides, and they suggested this could be a successful business venture. Thus, the seed of a business idea sprouted from my academic pursuit.

This was my comeback Number One! They say there is a light at the end of the tunnel. And so, just like that, with all that I had seen and experienced, somewhere, deep down, the idea had started.

Gap Year

After completing my college project, I found myself in a phase where I simply wanted to distance myself from anything related to architecture. I craved a break, and I decided to travel. I had to get a little extra crazy, you know, with all the feeling of liberation I had after completing my architecture.

I wanted to travel for three months. Convincing my father to provide additional funds for my travel adventure was a challenge, yet I managed to persuade him. I requested 30,000 INR, this time just for me and not for college or work. I did not attend my graduation ceremony and instead chose to celebrate in Goa. The whole idea of obtaining a degree, a mere piece of paper, seemed insignificant and futile in my eyes. It made me question the education system's structure and the obsession with a certificate that often goes underutilised.

Reflecting on this, I felt that if only our education system were more holistic, integrating elements of culture, mentorship, and practical knowledge, it would make more sense. The current system appeared more like a race where everyone was paying for an education that ultimately leads to a structured life of conformity. It feels like you pay to become a slave for life. It was a realisation that education could be so much more if it was aligned with practical wisdom and personal growth rather than just certification and institutional hierarchy.

I began to wonder how different things would have been for me had I discovered the Ashtavakra Gita or Bhagavad Gita much earlier. A lot of knowledge and information, if given at the right time, could help people grow so much faster. And that is exactly what I want to do as a coach. I wish to give all my fellow artists all the information and knowledge that I have gained and hold nothing back so we can all grow as a community.

After deciding to travel for three months, which cost 30,000 rupees ($360), I encountered a whole new dimension of learning. I decided that I would not be going back home anytime soon. Travelling with a friend from Scotland, I experienced the European perspective on travel, a concept that empowered me to value exploration and a 'Gap year,' which allows a pause for self-discovery.

I have noticed that not many of us Indians give that much importance and priority to travel. If you are reading this and you have a child who needs a break, or if you need a break for yourself, take it. I discovered that six months of travel provided more learning than six years of formal education.

Travelling taught me vital life skills like adapting to new environments, decision-making which will contribute to your leadership skills, budgeting, effective communication across cultures, and embracing diverse experiences. I realised that these skills are invaluable for personal growth and in the world of business.

If you want to be confident in the voice you wish to show the world, travel. My biggest message to anyone who wishes to become successful in life is to travel.

During my travels in South India, especially in Kochi during the Biennale, I encountered exceptional international artists. This exposure connected the dots between my quest for spirituality, self-discovery, and the realm of art. This realisation led to Revelation number three—the recognition that artists are Gods.

From Hi God, to Thank You God, to You are God!

This insight marked a significant shift in my thinking. I began seeing myself not just as someone seeking spirituality but also as someone capable of creating and shaping worlds through art. I felt inspired and influenced by the artists I encountered, igniting a desire to become an artist myself. This realisation marked the beginning of my aspiration to contribute to the world through art.

And I continued to travel. I went from Goa to Kochi and later to Ernakulam and Kanyakumari. It was a mesmerising journey through South India. I ventured further into Tamil Nadu, exploring Madurai, Kodaikanal, Kanchipuram, Chennai, and finally reaching the awe-inspiring Mahabalipuram.

Skill Exchange and Barter System:
I discovered that my skills were valuable even while travelling. Through the barter system, I exchanged my art skills for services, realising that offering value to people could fetch me food, accommodation, and various necessities. It taught me the significance of providing value in return for what I needed."

Financial Management and Decision-Making:
Backpacking taught me the essence of budgeting and making informed decisions. It showed me how to survive and thrive, even with limited financial resources, and instilled a valuable sense of financial prudence and independence."

Responsibility builds confidence:
Not everyone is born bold. It is something that we learn from making mistakes and taking responsibility for ourselves. It enhances confidence and self-assurance.

Real freedom lies beyond home:
True freedom is experienced when stepping out of the comfort of home—a vital life skill for independence. Parents provide protection, not freedom. Real freedom

comes from experiences outside the home.

Solo Travel: Never Alone:
Travelling solo teaches that friendships are formed along the journey, offering companionship even in solitude.

Now my journey of art started during these backpacking travels. Through skill exchange, I painted walls, managed cafes, and offered creative skills in return for accommodation and meals. I even found myself writing menus on a chalkboard in exchange for a good place to stay. All this, in India.

This proves that travelling on a budget is possible through exchanges. So if you are a teenager wondering how you can achieve your art dreams, let me tell you it is possible. You can travel on a budget with your skills.

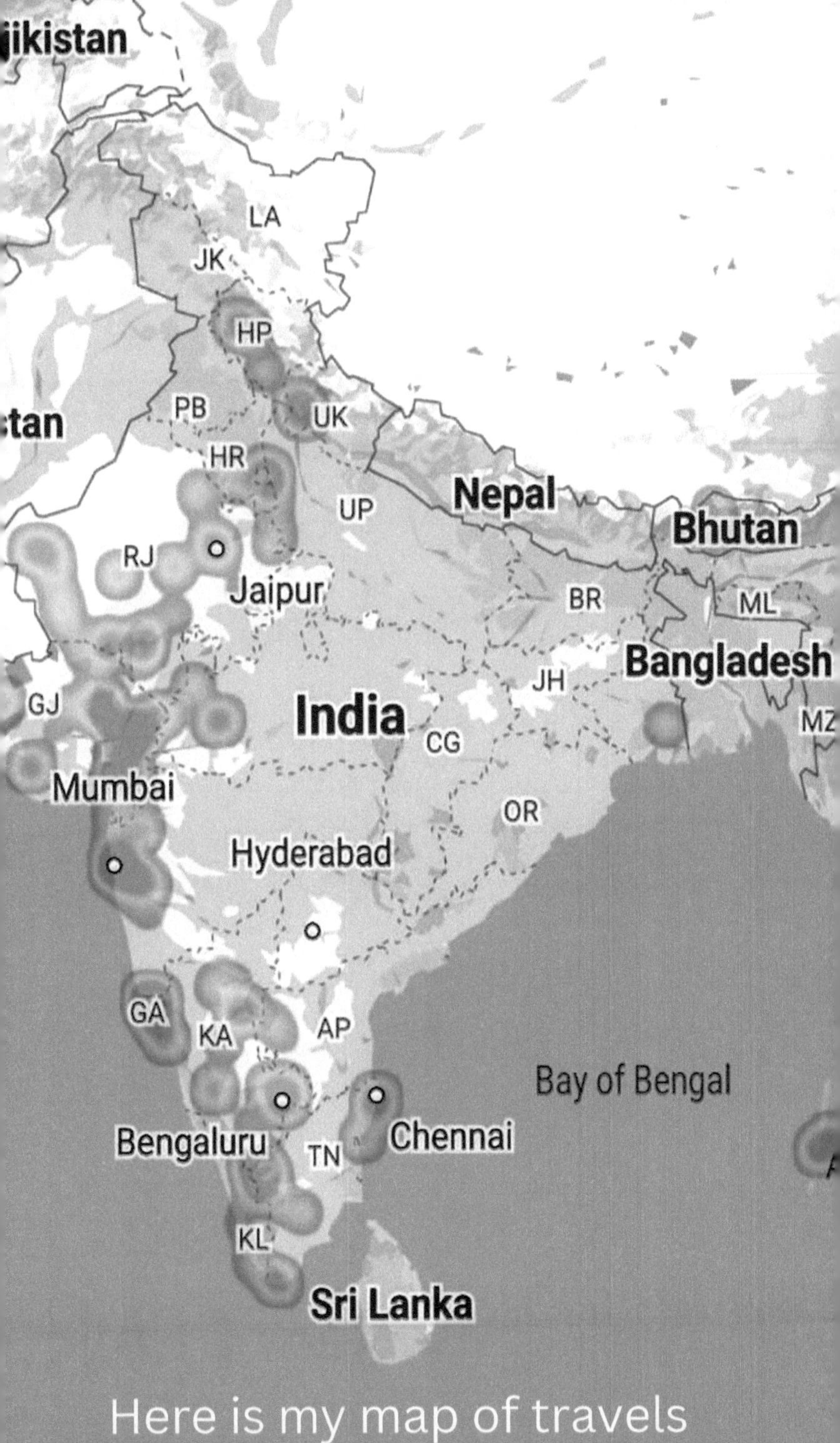
Tajikistan
Pakistan
LA
JK
HP
PB
UK
HR
UP
Nepal
Bhutan
RJ
Jaipur
BR
ML
Bangladesh
GJ
India
JH
MZ
CG
Mumbai
OR
Hyderabad
GA
KA
AP
Bay of Bengal
Bengaluru
TN
Chennai
KL
Sri Lanka
Here is my map of travels

My Heart Child

Coming back home after all that travelling, I did not feel like I belonged there anymore. You know that feeling when you have grown and seen so much? I did some pretty crazy stuff! From Madurai to Kodaikanal, I backpacked like a nomad and hopped three trucks and three cars just for a six-hour journey.

It reminded me of the movie 'Highway' in which the female protagonist travels in a truck. I probably looked even scruffier, though! When I look at all my pictures from those days, I think, 'Yep, I lived on the edge!' I was this skinny girl, lugging around a massive 90-litre backpack, climbing into trucks like, 'What in the world am I doing?' But hey, it is these wild tales that make life. I am sure I will pass these down to my future kids and tell them, 'This is how you live life to the fullest!'

The boundaries are what we create in our heads. Nature has no boundaries. Mountains, beaches—they don't sit around saying, *'I'm this'* or *'I'm that.'* It's just one big world!

We humans? We are the ones dividing it up, fighting over bits of land. Like, who are we kidding? We are just temporary tenants on this earth, thinking we own the place!

So these boundaries began to blur for me. It is funny how everything comes full circle. That whole thing about us being different is the biggest deception in the book! Those boundaries—I never really saw them. With all my friends scattered all over the world, from Scotland to Japan, Baroda to Jordan, Gulf countries, and Syria, my friend circle's like a UN summit! But hey, between us, there were no borders. We were just folks hanging out and sharing stories and vibes. But the world? It is all about those lines on the map. And you know what? All this mixing and mingling of cultures and people? And my art was happening simultaneously.

It was around this time that I got into another relationship, and this person played a significant role in my complete transition from an architect into an artist. He became a friend first, and then we started to date. Both of us had finished our graduation, and it felt like a more mature phase of life. We shared a passion for travelling and a love for food. He happened to be a chef, and he did know how to make me happy by feeding me! Food has always held a special place in my heart. Even today, my school is called FAT World School (Food, Art, and Travel, so they have always been very important to me). He just added more flavour to it all. It felt like I loved him the most; it was a beautiful journey.

I felt a newfound sense of maturity when experiencing love with someone. We travelled extensively, both of us trying to navigate our career paths and life's purpose. I am incredibly grateful for having such a supportive partner by my side.

While in Bhutan, something incredible happened. It was there that the idea of 'The Moving Artist' was born.

My partner suggested, 'Why not keep painting while you travel? Your story is fascinating—why not share it with the world through your art on Instagram?'

So, he helped me create a new page and gave life to the concept of 'The Moving Artist' on Instagram. Credit goes to him for urging me to showcase my art to the world. It was my 25th birthday when I launched my Instagram page, 'The Moving Artist.' It was a recent endeavour, something I decided to dive into at 25, to unveil my art to the world. 'The Moving Artist' was not just a brainchild; it was like something straight from my heart. It encapsulated my love for travel, food, and art, my 'heart child,' born from this passion for everything in life.

My 'heart child' eventually turned into my 'fat child' because I cared for it so deeply and nourished it with immense love. This brand, which I poured my heart and soul into, faced a challenging period after the breakup. Life took a turn despite having an incredible and supportive partner, leading us down separate paths due to our differences and insecurities. However, amidst this, he gave me something precious—the idea to start my 'heart child.'

Following the breakup, I found myself in a sort of mini-depression, overwhelmed by emotions. During this time, I turned to painting, and for 21 consecutive days, I expressed my emotions through abstract art. It was a significant shift for 'The Moving Artist'. I was not moving physically; instead, I was at home, broken-hearted, yet expressing myself. Each day, painting made me feel a bit better, gradually pulling me out of that emotional state.

You know, they say that if you do something for 21 days straight, it becomes a habit. It is a lesson they teach us in school. I started painting every day for 21 days, considering myself a bit of an artist. And after those 21 days, I had created 21 paintings.

Surprisingly, by the end of this consistent routine, something magical happened. I sold one of my artworks for 7,000 INR! It was a turning point in my life, a game-changer. Despite my heartbreak, expressing myself through art brought me money.

That moment made me realise that continuing with this could be worthwhile. It was a tough time; my parents were also pushing me after wasting a year on a gap year and a failed attempt at something else.

They kept asking, '*What are you doing with your life?*'

That was when I decided firmly that I was going to paint. 'The Moving Artist' was not just a passion; it became the brand I was determined to build. I never saw myself as just an artist; I envisioned it as a brand from the start.

My focus was always on building my brand rather than solely on myself. The idea of a business mindset was rooted deep within me, though I never pursued things solely for gain. Emotions always took centre stage for me. I have always been and will continue to be an emotional person. Money or business never held the spotlight. It was all about expression.

I was always focused on building my brand rather than solely on myself. The idea of a business mindset was rooted deep within me, though I never pursued things solely for gain. Emotions always took centre stage for me; I have always been and will continue to be an emotional person. Money or business never held the spotlight—it was all about expression.

After the initial 21 days, I kept creating more and more art until I filled an entire room with it! I still have stacks of art waiting to be shared. My memory of when my art started getting bigger is a bit hazy, but what I do recall is the consistency of sharing on Instagram.

That is secret number one. Staying consistent on one platform. Interestingly, I had close ties with the architecture faculty and fellow graduates. The first person who did this was Sandeep.

Sandeep, who was a friend and is still a friend, owns a furniture showroom in Bangalore. His purchase was a significant validation for me; a professional endorsing my art gave me confidence. It meant my work was valued at a professional level. Throughout my journey, I drew inspiration from abstract artists. I never felt jealous of them, or I never envied them.

I always believed I was creating something unique and magical; I never thought I was bad at it. Each day, I painted a large piece, usually 2'x3' or 3'x3, and as I finished each artwork, I was in a state of wonder more than competition. I wondered how I managed to balance these artworks so well. It felt almost like a divine channelling of talent.

Painting and sharing on Instagram became a ritual. I used to religiously paint and post every day on Instagram. It became a daily practice, and I never shied away from criticism. I loved all the appreciation I received from everyone online for my artwork.

In my life, my family, especially my brother, Utkarsh, and my father, were my biggest critics. It was typical brotherly behaviour—utterly unable to express any praise, even if they felt it. I could see the delight in my brother's expression when he saw my art, but his words were always the opposite.

Yet I want to thank him, my biggest critic, to show that he, too, has been instrumental in my journey. Then there is my father, the second biggest critic, a scientific mind working in nuclear power who could spot a flaw in my art from miles away; *'rejected'* became his signature review for my pieces. Neither of them knew much about art, but their criticism, though sometimes disheartening, pushed me to paint more and master my craft. I owe a lot to these not-so-supportive men in my life, for their criticism, in its own way, made me strive for excellence. Constructive criticism, even from unlikely sources, is what helps us grow. We need them.

Here is a task for you. Pick your favourite topic or medium of art, take up the 21-Day Art Task for Today (ATT Challenge), and work on it consistently. You will be surprised at how much you have progressed in the past 21 days. We do it often at my school, and the results I have seen in my community are only more proof that it is an effective method to build your art skills.

And so it begins

People saw my art on Instagram, and I started receiving significant appreciation. Surprisingly, within a short span of maybe three months, I gained a thousand followers. It was rapid growth for me, and my art was gradually becoming more popular.

Oh, I recall now, during my backpacking journey in South India, I met a group of boys during my journey in South India, and one of them took an interest in my Instagram page. He invited me to visit Coimbatore and assist in his venture, a café targeting the urban crowd, built entirely from sustainable materials.

They aimed to combine art and architecture, seeking my input for this unique fusion. Everything from tickets, and accommodations, to all the necessities was sponsored for me to contribute my creative imagination. It was my first client experience, all made possible because of art showcased on Instagram.

And then the most significant moment in my life unfolded. One day, the client's children and I were having fun, playing around with some art materials. It was a happy, creative day.

I stumbled upon this art form that I had been seeing on Instagram. It looked so enjoyable and flowy that I was determined to give it a try. Strangely, in India, I could not find anyone teaching or practicing this technique. No one guided me; I just decided to experiment. I mixed acrylics, Fevicol (white glue), and water. It might sound odd, but it was an idea sparked by childhood memories of transparent Fevicol.

Remember the joy of peeling it off your skin as a kid? It struck me that when applied to the skin, it turned transparent. So I thought, 'Why not mix it with colours?' I adjusted the consistency, aiming for something akin to Dosa batter—you know, South India, Dosa batter consistency! Miraculously, this 'Dosa batter consistency' turned out to be the perfect blend of materials. That is how we created our first masterpiece on a 2'x3' canvas with the kids, all sponsored by my client.

On this big canvas, we poured those mixed colours, and as a team, we created a breathtaking fluid art masterpiece. The painting went viral, and people started requesting that I teach this new form of artwork —fluid art.

Requests poured in from Chennai, Coimbatore, and Bangalore, and gigs started coming my way. It was the power of social media, fueled by consistent postings for at least a year. I found myself sponsored once again, a trend that was becoming the norm in my life. Flight tickets, accommodations, and even payment to teach art I had discovered while having fun with kids—it was like being hired to have fun. I felt like I had the best job ever.

But it was not just about the fun; it was realising my love for teaching and the purpose of sharing joy through art with the world. I saw that a lot of people, especially those who were working corporate jobs, needed an outlet and needed therapy.

More than the money I was making from it, it was the smiles I saw, which were truly priceless. With each teaching session in different cities, amidst diverse cultures, I witnessed art uniting everyone, transcending language barriers solely through joy, bliss, and smiles. It became clear: I would not stop teaching if it meant bringing happiness to people.

Reaching the pinnacle of my art career, I found myself continuously invited to conduct art workshops, meet countless people, and enjoy the freedom to spend my earnings as I pleased. I was making 50,000 to 70,000 a month, getting to do what I wanted to. I was young, and this lifestyle was thrilling. I partied, made friends, and travelled across different cities for my workshops. I also got to meet many famous artists.

However, after a taxing workshop day, as I returned, I realised the toll it took on me. While initially, these gigs were all paid for and managed by others.

Although content with the money and lifestyle, I began seeking ways to maximise my profits. Balancing the effort required to please everyone and retain my own energy levels became challenging. Often, after witnessing smiles and laughter, I would return home too exhausted to celebrate or even gather energy for myself.

I realised the need to secure more income, not just to rest but also to celebrate my own successes. As artists, we often prioritise satisfying our clients to the point of draining ourselves. I am sure that if you, too, have already started to sell artwork to clients, you would have done the same at some point.

I learned the importance of preserving and respecting our artistic gifts while always striving to share them with our best energy. Sometimes, it is crucial to postpone or delay when we are not in our best state to ensure we give our best. You can allow yourself to do that.

Because when you are drained, you cannot give your best. So there I was, exhausted and tired after all the workshops and parties. I earned some money, spent it lavishly, and found myself flying back to Gujarat. Every time I returned home, I vividly remembered my mother laughing at me, saying, 'You've spent all your money again, haven't you?'

She was right—I was a terrible money manager. I'd spend everything I had, and when it came to reaching home from the airport, I would end up borrowing the last 200 or 300 rupees ($4) from my mother for a cab. Perhaps saving was not my priority; I just wanted to live life to the fullest. But truth be told, I was awful at money management. I am still trying to work on this aspect of my life. I tend to spend a lot, and sometimes in my business ventures, money seems to vanish without a trace. It's perplexing—expenses just seem to pile up.

Alright! We have now reached the end of our drive and are at the foot of the mountain we are going to hike. It is going to be quite the climb. Imagine the success of your art business is at the summit.

Now as we climb, one stretch at a time, I will continue telling you my story and share what I learned in the process. Each step we take will be a step closer to your success. We will look at how you could benefit from the same. We might do an exercise or two on the way, too.

You can hold my hand as we go higher. Do not worry. I will be here with you to guide you. Have you geared up? So it begins.

The Gentleman on the Flight

During my journey of poor money management and carefree living, I had a significant encounter on a flight from Bangalore to Gujarat. I met this man, the corporate capitalist type, who seemed initially unapproachable. He was pretty curt to the airline staff, and I hesitated to engage with him. I intended to just sleep through the flight.

However, he eventually greeted me, and our conversation began. We shall call him Vision Uncle.

He asked, 'Are you happy doing what you're doing?'

I replied enthusiastically about feeling blessed and lucky. I quickly filled him in on what I was doing and my brand. He then asked about the vision I had for my brand, The Moving Artist. I had no solid answers. His next question was about what my mission was. Gaian, I had no answers. In my head, I was thinking about how I wanted to just fly to places and keep creating art. I was simply living day-by-day, enjoying travel and painting, with no defined dreams or goals. This question lingered in my mind for months, urging me to contemplate the vision for my life's work.

It took me quite some time to realise what I truly envisioned for myself. Initially, it was about making people smile, but the deeper question remained: 'Where do you want to go?' After much contemplation, I realised that I was tired of doing things for others. The vision began to transform within me. I wanted to embark on a journey for myself.

Before we go further into my story, let us look at your vision and mission. It is alright if you do not have it planned already. In the following chapter, you will learn how to find your vision and mission in your art journey and their importance. Come hold my hand as we take this step.

Discovering your artistic vision and mission

The Essence of Your Artistic Purpose:

One of the terms used for this is ikigai. It is not just a concept; it is at the core of your successful and fulfilling artistic journey. It comprises everything: your passion, expertise, societal demand, and financial viability.

In the context of artists, it is finding that sweet spot where your love for creation meets the world's hunger for art that helps show you the direction that you need to be taking.

Here is an exercise I would like for you to do now:

Grab a book and a pen or pencil, take a moment to contemplate, and answer the following:
- What do you love most about creating art?
- What are you truly exceptional at in your

artistic realm?
- What does the world yearn for in the world of art?
- How can you balance these aspects to make a sustainable living through art?

You now have a clearer picture of how and what you think is needed out there, which only you can give. It can be something that someone is already doing, but only you can give it your touch.

Self-Reflection and Introspection: The Pillars of Artistic Self-Discovery:
Let yourself dive deep within; look at who you are at the core of yourself. It is like uncovering the rare gems that define you as an artist. Because there is only one you, and only you can create your art. Introspecting like this can act as a compass, one that guides you to your north: your passions and strengths.

Now try doing this exercise: Artistic Self-Reflection Consider and document the following:
- The fondest memories of creating art from your past.
- Instances where your artistic work received high praise or recognition.
- The subjects or themes that consistently ignite a fire within you.
- The techniques or mediums that feel most natural and enjoyable to you.

Answering these questions will help solidify what you really feel connected to in terms of your subject, style, and medium.

Exploring Your Artistic Passions: Fuel for Your Creative Fire

Passion can be considered the rocket fuel propelling artists to reach celestial heights. As dramatic as that sounds, it is true. Passion is everything when it comes to creating art.

Passion for the art form, for your subject, for how it makes you feel—while thinking of it, while creating it in your head or physically, while finishing it—is what makes all the difference. Can you imagine making something just for the sake of being made to do it? Do you think you would be satisfied with the outcome, as opposed to something that you made that your heart craved to make?

Passion is what adds soul to your art. Any piece of artwork created from within the heart is a masterpiece. It is about identifying that which makes your heart beat faster in the realm of art.

Let us find out what you are truly passionate about with this exercise: Passion Profiling

Go back to your notebook.
Create a list of your top artistic passions.
Mediums you're most passionate about (e.g., oil

painting, sculpture, digital art).
Themes that stir a deep emotional response within you.
Artistic styles that resonate with your soul.

Now, taking me as an example again, I wish to empower women. I want to help animals. I love art and the freedom it gives. I love to travel and eat, so I can connect. well with any of these topics. Getting to know this will help you understand your heart's calling.

Unveiling Your Strengths: The Arsenal of an Artistic Virtuoso

Acknowledging your strengths and talents is fundamental. As an artist, there will be certain skills and strong points that you know you possess. Let go of all other thoughts, be true to yourself, and find out and accept those things that you are genuinely good at. Because self-awareness is necessary here. Mastery of these strengths distinguishes you in the art world.

Time for another exercise:
Strength Identification
List at least five of your artistic strengths: Skills you've honed over time (e.g., brushwork, composition, storytelling).
Unique qualities that set you apart as an artist (e.g., attention to detail, innovative thinking).

For example, I know that I am good at communication. I am good at designing; I am an architect; I have a good aesthetic sense; and I can connect to people's emotions, so I am empathetic. I can bring all of these into my art.

Having answered this to yourself, you are more aware of your strengths. This is what you are going to contribute to the art world that is not there yet. And it is something only you can do.

Aligning with a Purpose: How Your Art Can Serve a Higher Calling

Your art can have a larger purpose. Through your art, you can influence society and touch hearts. Once you put it out there, it has the ability to make an impression on people. It is like music; it has the ability to transcend language barriers and speak to so many people from everywhere. This is where the magic happens—when your artistic expression serves a higher cause.

Exercise: Artistic Purpose Alignment
Contemplate and document:
How can your art provoke emotions or thoughts in the viewers?
In what ways can your artistic work contribute positively to society or individuals?
How can you align your passion, strengths, and purpose into a single artistic vision?

In my case, I am very passionate about teaching what I know, sharing it with people, and helping them grow as artists and in their businesses. Again, here I can combine my passions, strengths, and style and understand what I can get paid.

Merging Passion, Vocation, Profession, and Mission: Forging Your Ikigai Statement

As a final step in this chapter, we will now craft your artist's Ikigai Statement. It comprises your passion, vocation, profession, and mission in the artistic realm, all put together. When all of the above combine, you have it.

Do not be in a hurry, and think well as you do this exercise: Crafting Your Ikigai Statement
Formulate a crisp Ikigai statement by putting together all that you discovered from the exercises you did earlier.
Combine your passions, strengths, and purpose into a clear, powerful Ikigai statement that fuels your artistic journey.

My artist statement will be something along the lines of, "I would like to empower 1,00,000 women through art in the next 5 years."

Your artistic destiny awaits.
By delving into your Ikigai, you have set the stage for an extraordinary artistic venture. You have a

clear map of what and why you are doing what you are doing with your art. Your Ikigai will be your guiding light, propelling you towards unparalleled success and fulfilment as an artist. All the very best, and with this clarity, let us move on to the next chapter, wherein we discuss one of the very common but strong challenges every artist faces in some form at some point in their artistic journey.

Finally, some
direction

Getting back to my story, after my encounter with that gentleman, I underwent a transformation in my approach. I realised that while travelling brought opportunities, being home in Vadodara allowed me to leverage my networks and generate more income. I observed that I could earn more by organising workshops at home compared to when I was travelling. This realisation birthed the solopreneur mindset within me. I decided to start arranging workshops on my own turf, maximising profits.

These workshops became a hit. I received numerous offers, some paying up to one lakh a day for organising fluid art workshops. The trend caught on in Gujarat, and I gained recognition as an expert in the field of fluid art. The Moving Artist became increasingly popular. I recall an incident where I was strolling down the streets, and someone greeted me as 'Moving Artist.' While it felt odd that they forgot my name (Rashmi), it was a testament that the brand was making its mark.

Now, I found immense satisfaction in building my brand and reputation, earning far more at home than when I worked for others. I maintained my freedom to travel wherever I desired while still making money. I mastered the art of earning income wherever I went. This marked a new chapter in my life. People began inviting me to various places and offering opportunities for workshops, and I capitalised on this by leveraging my skills in organising and managing these events independently.

I learned the ropes of running my business autonomously. Moreover, I received commissions for artwork from architects due to my rising popularity and the trust I built by consistently delivering quality work.

At this point, I found a new way to earn money by creating art pieces that people specifically asked for. I spent time crafting a series of artworks for my upcoming exhibition. The first opportunity to display my creations came from the architecture community itself. They kindly invited me to showcase my artwork in their space. This experience reinforced the idea that starting from familiar territory, like home, holds a special value. It is where I found my footing, gained support, and felt most confident in launching my artistic journey.

Now, with some fictional examples, I would like to introduce another very important set of lessons I have learned so far in my journey.

The Power Principles to Start a Smart Business

With any business you do, there are certain power principles that you must follow in order to get the most out of it. In this chapter, we will be looking at what you must focus on and how you must go about doing certain things in your business. Let us not wait any further and delve into the following list:.

Authenticity and a unique voice:

"To be yourself in a world that is constantly trying to make you something else is the greatest achievement".
- Ralph Waldo Emerson

Authenticity is the most important aspect of your business. Because that is what sets you apart from everyone else—the originality that you can offer. You have to stay true to who you are, your voice, and your unique vision, and express all of these through your creations. People will be attracted to your work because of that.

Now let us take Ishani, a budding artist who wanted to carve a niche in the art world, for example. As she started, she was confused. She was torn between following popular trends and staying true to her unique artistic style. She tried following the crowd. But she could not connect with it at all. It seemed to be missing something.

After giving it some thought, she realised that there was no soul in it. So she decided to do what she genuinely wanted to do: follow her style, trust her heart, and create. Soon, there were people interested in knowing more about what was put out there. Why? Because they were intrigued. It was unique. Because only Sarah could do Ishani's style.

She realised that embracing her authentic voice was the key to creating art that resonated deeply with her and her audience. As she stayed true to herself, her work gained recognition, and she became a celebrated artist known for her distinctive style.

Therefore, if you have any second thoughts about doing what you want to do, this is your cue. Just do it. Unlike Sarah, you will not be wasting your time trying to do what everyone is doing. Authenticity builds a genuine connection with your audience, fostering trust and loyalty.

Market Research and Target Audience:

"Research is to see what everybody else has seen and to think what nobody else has thought."
- Albert Szent-Gyorgyi

When you decide to sell your art, you need to know who you are selling it to. Think about who your target customers are. You need to know your market well. So thorough market research is vital. You have to understand:
Art market dynamics,
The preferences of your buyers, and
Demographics.

Identify who your target audience is, customise your art accordingly, and plan your outreach messages with them in mind. Have effective marketing strategies ready.

Let us look at David, an artist who spent time studying art market trends and understanding what his potential buyers were looking for. Through meticulous research, he learned to align his artwork with market demands. He analysed their feedback, considered their preferences, and tailored his artwork to attract his target audience. This resulted in an increase in his sales and satisfied, happy customers.

Knowing your audience ensures your art

resonates with those most likely to appreciate and purchase it.

Professional Branding:

"Your brand is what people say about you when you're not in the room.'
- Jeff Bezos

Your brand has to define who you are and has to speak for you. You need to craft a professional brand identity that covers everything: your style, your values, and your story. It should, at a glance, communicate what it is that sets you apart from the rest of the crowd and leaves a lasting impression on your target audience.

To understand how it works, let us take Priya, a talented painter, for example. Priya was set with what she was going to sell, her style, and everything else that was required. Now it was time for her to design her brand identity. She wanted it to reflect her passion for nature and her love for vibrant colours.

So, she put in the effort, dedicated the required amount of time, and thought into designing how her branding would look on various platforms and media. This can be on a banner, visiting cards, or product labels. pamphlets, portfolios, social media platforms, letterheads, and just about anywhere.

Her consistent branding across various platforms showed her unique style, and over time, people recognised her work even without her signature, establishing a strong brand presence and a devoted following.

So create your branding mindfully because your brand is going to live on for a very long time. While designing it, keep in mind the possibility of expansion in the future and allow for flexibility. A strong brand attracts the right audience and instills confidence in your work.

Diverse Portfolio:

"Diversity is not about how we differ. Diversity is about embracing one another's uniqueness"
- Ola Joseph.

As an artist, you have to have a portfolio that shows what kind of work you do. Your portfolio is what you will send out to your clients, sometimes even before meeting them in person. So, in a way, it could be your first point of contact with them, responsible for the first impression you make on them. Therefore, just like how you carefully plan your branding, you have to pay attention to what goes in your portfolio as well.

This may get you wondering what exactly you should add to your portfolio. I have you covered. It has to be diverse. You may be an artist who has a set style that you try on various mediums, or you may like to work on a specific medium but experiment with various styles using that one medium. Or, you may be a mixed-media artist. Whatever it is, showcase a diverse portfolio that highlights your versatility and capabilities. But at the same time, avoid going overboard, keeping it harmonious, and not making it confusing. Each page and everything in your portfolio should complement the other.

For example, Arjun, an aspiring sculptor, liked to experiment with various sculpting materials and styles. So, he showed exactly that. By showing how versatile he was in his art, he attracted a wider audience who appreciated different forms of creativity. His diverse portfolio became a testament to the beauty of embracing uniqueness in art.

From different mediums to various subjects, a diverse portfolio demonstrates your range and captures the interest of a broader audience. Diversity keeps your audience excited and intrigued.

Quality and Excellence:

"Quality is never an accident. It is always the result of high intention, sincere effort, intelligent direction, and

skillful execution.' - William. A.Foster

Quality has to be good, and it goes without saying. When you provide good-quality work, your credibility as an artist naturally gets cemented. There should be no compromises in the quality you provide. This includes everything: the materials you use, the way you present your work, the packaging, your interaction with your customers, the service you provide, and so on.

We shall look at Ananya, a meticulous artist who always emphasised quality. She paid attention to every detail, ensuring her artwork reflected excellence. She maintained putting out only good-quality work out there, and over time, her commitment to it paid off. Art enthusiasts began recognising and valuing her exceptional craftsmanship, establishing her as a respected artist.

When you are planning anything, simply put yourself in your customer's shoes and ask yourself if you would like it. When you uphold unwavering standards of quality in every aspect of your art business, artwork, and customer service, your customers will simply keep coming back to you for more because they trust you and your word. They know that investing in it, in you, is worth it. Delivering excellence in all you do establishes a solid foundation for long-term success.

Effective Marketing Strategies:

"Doing business without advertising is like winking at a girl in the dark. You know what you are doing, but nobody else does." - Steuart Henderson Britt

Marketing has to be a part of your business strategy. You have to let people know what you are doing. And that has to be done effectively. You can employ a mix of effective marketing strategies customised to your target audience. Use social media, email campaigns, collaborations, exhibitions, and more.

Let us take another example for this: Kabir, an aspiring digital artist, learned the importance of marketing his creations effectively. Through strategic online promotions and engaging social media campaigns, he let his artwork be seen by the entire world. This exposure led to increased visibility, a surge in followers, and a steady growth in sales.

Strategic marketing ensures your art reaches the right audience at the right time, amplifying your reach and impact. You have to be consistent and know your audience, where they are more likely to look, and target those platforms especially.

Engagement and relationship building:

"The art of communication is the language of leadership."
-James Humes

You have to engage with your audience regularly and interact with them. They need to know that you see them and value them. Being seen and heard makes them feel valued. Try to respond to them promptly, share your insights, have interactive polls, and provide value to them. You have to make them feel eager to come and visit your page and your website and keep them there.

This brings us to our next artist, Neha, a talented illustrator who understood that art is not just about drawing but also about connecting with the audience. She engaged her audience through live sessions and art workshops. In doing so, she forged a sense of community. This interactive approach enriched her relationships, and her art became a language that spoke to many.

Building genuine relationships fosters a community around your art, leading to loyal customers who also become advocates of your brand. That kind of human connection matters.

Pricing strategy:

"Price is what you pay; value is what you get."
-Warren Buffet

A lot has to be considered while planning your pricing. It has to balance your artistic value and market demand. There are quite a few factors you must include while doing so, must include while doing so, some of which are:
- Production Costs
- Time invested and
- Your brand's reputation.

This can get a little confusing and intimidating because it may seem a little difficult to determine the cost of art, unlike other products one can easily compare the prices of competitors with. However, that is why I am here. And in order to convince your clients that they are paying the right amount, you need to convince yourself of the same and accept it in your mind first.

Let us look at Krish, a skilled photographer who learned that pricing his art is an art in itself. He focused on showcasing the value of his photography through storytelling and personalised experiences. People need to understand that what they get from your art is not just a mere picture; there has to be an emotional connection to it, and that will make a lot of difference. And that is what

Krish did. By effectively communicating the worth of his work, he attracted buyers willing to invest in the unique value he offered.

When it is well thought out, your pricing strategy ensures your art is priced competitively and appropriately.

Efficient Operations:

"Efficiency is doing things right; effectiveness is doing the right things.'
- Peter Drucker

Streamline your operations from creation to delivery. As an artist, creating your art in itself will take up a lot of your time. There are no shortcuts to any creative process. If you do everything from creating art, content for your social handles to managing your social media, responding to every interaction you get on your posts, and packing and shipping all by yourself, you will have difficulty managing your time. If you have already been doing this, you know how overwhelming it can get sometimes, especially when you have to meet deadlines. This will directly reflect on your artwork. So, what do you do?

Let us go back to Ishani, whom we saw earlier. She was aware of this, and so she streamlined her art business operations, organising her studio and automating administrative tasks. By doing so, she was able to dedicate more time to her art and less time to administrative hassles. This helped her find a balance that allowed her to create exceptional artwork.

So all you have to do is implement efficient processes for art creation, inventory management, sales, and customer service. A well-organised operation ensures a smooth and professional experience for your customers.

Financial literacy and management:

"Financial literacy is not an end in itself but a step-by-step process. It begins with understanding how money works and how to make it work for you. - Robert Kiyosaki.

It is one thing to make money, but it is a whole other thing to manage it well. You need to acquire the financial knowledge that is crucial to managing your art business efficiently. Because you are also a businessperson, not only an artist. Though your job as an artist is to create art, you also need to be able to keep your art business running smoothly.

Rohan, an aspiring sculptor, recognised the importance of financial literacy quite early in his career. He sought advice from financial experts, learned about investments, and managed his earnings wisely. By making informed financial decisions, he ensured the sustainability and growth of his art business.

Any business will have its ups and downs, and the art business is no different. Therefore, understanding budgeting, cash flow, pricing, and taxes will help you prepare for the financial challenges that may crop up. Sound financial management lays the groundwork for a sustainable and profitable art business.

Continuous learning and growth:

"The only limit to our realisation of tomorrow will be our doubts of today.'
- Franklin D.Roosevelt

Stay hungry for knowledge and growth. You have to continuously educate yourself on art trends, business strategies, and technological advancements. The world is growing at an unimaginable pace. Things that were only dreamed of or joked about are now real. So it is very important that you keep yourself updated on what's happening in the art world and be open to learning new skills at every opportunity you get.

Michelle, a dedicated painter, understood that learning is a lifelong journey. She attended workshops, collaborated with fellow artists, and sought inspiration from various art forms. Embracing a growth mindset, she constantly evolved and improved her art, surprising herself with what she could achieve.

Continually educate yourself on art trends, business strategies, and technological advancements. This will also let you avoid feeling saturated or your work getting monotonous. Learning something new every once in a while will make the process more exciting and keep your passion alive. A commitment to lifelong learning keeps you relevant and evolving in the dynamic art industry.

Networking and Collaboration:

"Alone, we can do so little; together, we can do so much.' Helen Keller.

Being an artist is considered to be a lonely job. It is just you and your art in your studio. Sounds lovely. However, this can also lead to isolation. This is where connecting with like-minded people helps. Networking actively within your art community and beyond will help you in more ways than you can think of.

That is what happened with Arjun, a talented graphic designer who actively networked with artists, designers, and art enthusiasts. Collaborating on projects enhanced his creativity and exposed his work to new audiences. These collaborations not only enriched his portfolio but also broadened his horizons within the art community.

Because when you network, you obviously meet more people who may do something similar to what you do or something that complements what you do. When you collaborate and support each other, not only is your art growing in style, but so is the exposure that your work gets.

For example, if you have 500 followers and your new artist friend has 500 followers, your art gets exposed to 500 new people, and it is the same for the other person too. Besides, it is definitely more fun and nice to have one or more people with you working together. So go out there, find those communities, groups etc, and forge relationships with fellow artists, galleries and collectors, and industry professionals. Collaboration opens doors to new opportunities and gives more exposure and invaluable insights.

Persistence and resilience:

"Perseverance is not a long race. It is many short races one after another.' - Walter Elliot

Choosing a career as an artist can be a little scary. It is quite unconventional, and there are many who still think that it is a very risky choice to make in terms of financial stability. I know that there are quite a number of us who might have heard at least one or two people ask us if we were doing the right thing by making this choice. And I will not lie, it does come with its own set of challenges. But what does not? Everything has its pros and cons. What is more important is that you persevere through the setbacks.

Vikram, like many artists, faced numerous rejections early in his career. However, he persevered, learning from each setback. His determination and resilience fueled his passion for art, and eventually, his art gained him recognition. The challenging journey taught him that success often comes to those who keep going.

So it is alright if you come across a few roadblocks; they will someday inspire you. Just do not give up. Persistence, coupled with resilience, allows you to bounce back stronger and more determined. In the face of adversity, maintain focus on your goals, and keep moving forward.

Customer Centric Approach:

"Your most unhappy customers are your greatest source of learning." - Bill Gates

Your business should revolve around your

customers, so place them at the centre of your business strategy. Understand their needs, preferences, and feedback. Tweak your business strategy to fit them.

Tamara, a skilled illustrator, valued her customer feedback immensely. She actively sought input from her buyers and incorporated their suggestions into her work. By placing her customers at the core of her business, she not only satisfied them but also built a loyal customer base that eagerly awaited her new releases.

Tailor your art and services to meet and exceed customer expectations, fostering long-term relationships.

Passion and Dedication:

"Passion is energy. Feel the power that comes from focusing on what excites you.'
-Oprah Winfrey.

Let your passion drive your dedication to success. Pour your heart and soul into your craft. Let your authentic self show, and be vulnerable to your thoughts and emotions while you create your art. Dev's love for sculpting drove him to dedicate endless hours to perfecting the craft. His passion for creating intricate sculptures was reflected in his work, captivating art enthusiasts. His dedication to his art transformed his passion into a fulfilling and successful art business.

 There may be many instances where you second-guess your choice. It is okay; let those thoughts come and go. But every time that happens, remind yourself why you are doing this. Remind yourself of the passion you have for your art. Dedicate time and effort to continuously refine your skills, innovate, and elevate your art to new heights. Passion fuels your artistic journey and sets the stage for a fulfilling art business.

 Now that you know what the power principles are, we shall look at the mindset that you must cultivate to run a successful art business.

Home ground is the
best ground to
start from

Now that you know the power principles to start a smart business, let us continue to the next part of my journey that taught me more lessons. This one is quite important.

This is where the real-art journey took off. It all began in my hometown. Initially, people tend to gift you a lot of opportunities and recognition, especially in your own town. The real story of my art journey started right at home. I was given the chance to host a solo art show at my architecture college. I was quite nervous because it was going to be my first solo show. It was an incredible opportunity because the audience, fellow architects, were essentially my direct customers. They were the ones who would appreciate and potentially buy my art. The support and love I received were overwhelming.

Although I only sold one painting, it was an acknowledgement from the department that even architects could become artists, emphasising that anyone can become an artist. I am deeply grateful for the strong foundation provided by Maharaja Sayajirao University, my college of architecture. Our university is renowned for its rich cultural heritage, making us the cultural capital of Gujarat. It is among the top universities, and its commitment to education is exceptional. The affordable fees make it possible for anyone to excel here. The foundations laid during my college days kept me grounded, teaching us everything from the basics to the advanced skills needed to succeed. Many of my friends and colleagues from college are doing amazing things in the field, some working with renowned architects like Norman Foster and others having their own spaces featured in magazines.

The college's support was instrumental, and I owe a special mention to one person, Professor Mayur Gupta. He taught us basic design and was more than a mentor; he provided critique, support, and love. He saw me as a daughter, and we share a special bond. I affectionately call him 'Baba,' which means father. He was my initial guiding force as an artist, a true godfather figure.

I never considered myself an artist initially—I was

pursuing architecture. However, the influence of Baba transformed me into an artist. He encouraged me to follow my heart and was a true artist at heart. Baba is a bit eccentric, passionate about teaching, and adores children. He has only one daughter, and he treats me like one too, as we are around the same age. I deeply appreciate his constant support. I know I can always count on him; just one call away, he is there for me. His artwork is incredible, and he has even exhibited in New York—an international artist with amazing talent.

So, after organising that solo show, Baba's support was a game-changer for me. His advice about embracing my true self was a real eye-opener. His influence truly helped shape who I am today. Thanks to his guidance, my business took off. I was bringing in a steady income of around 40,000 to 50,000 bucks by hosting workshops just twice a month. That is more than what many earn from a gruelling 9-to-5 job. And it only took me two to three days each time. Plus, having local celebrities join my workshops added even more buzz to the scene!

We dabbled a bit in paid advertising, but most of our success came from networking and collaborations.

Alright, time for my next takeaway. This is where I learned a very big lesson. This is something I am sure most, if not all, artists go through. So you will have to hold my hand firmly as we take this next large step. Trust me, it is a big one. Because it involves fighting yourself to some extent. It requires consistency and commitment. Now, with this in mind, let us move higher.

Imposter Syndrome

Beating Doubt: Conquering the Artist's Inner Critic

Conquering Imposter Syndrome: Liberating the Artist Within:

As an artist, at many stages in your career, or the period preceding that, you might have subjected yourself to some form of self-doubt in regards to your artwork, skills, and where you are in your art journey. This is known as Imposter Syndrome.

Imposter syndrome is a relentless foe that many artists grapple with in their creative journeys, and it is the subject of this very important chapter. As your dedicated art business coach, I shed light on this common struggle and provide you with empowering strategies to overcome it, allowing you to embrace your true artistic potential.

1. Understanding Imposter Syndrome: The Silent Plague of Artists

Imposter syndrome is more prevalent than you might think. In a study published by the International Journal of Behavioral Science, it was revealed that an estimated 70% of individuals experience imposter feelings at some point in their lives. For artists, this phenomenon often manifests as a nagging self-doubt, despite their talent and achievements. So if you have ever found yourself thinking along those lines, do not worry; you are not alone. Recognising that you're not alone in this struggle is the first step towards liberation.

The Four Faces of Imposter Syndrome: Recognising the Enemy

Imposter syndrome often wears various masks, each presenting unique challenges.
- The 'Perfectionist' expects flawless execution,
- The 'Expert' fears exposure of inadequacy,
- The 'Natural Genius' dreads effort, and
- The 'Superman or Superwoman' believes they should excel in every role.

Identifying which face of Imposter Syndrome you wear empowers you to challenge and conquer it.

The Psychological Impact: How Imposter Syndrome Affects Your Artistic Journey

Imposter syndrome can hinder creativity, stifle innovation, and lead to anxiety and stress. It may discourage you from taking risks, showcasing your work, or pursuing opportunities that could elevate your career. It slows you down. Understanding the psychological toll it takes is crucial to breaking free from its clutches.

Breaking the Chains: Strategies to Conquer Imposter Syndrome

Having recognised, accepted, and understood Imposter Syndrome and the kind of effects it has on our work and our way of thinking, we will not take the second step towards conquering it.

This is what you can do.

- **Acknowledge and normalise:** Understand that it is okay to feel this way. Thoughts come and go, and these are also the same. Normalise these feelings and remind yourself that even successful artists have faced and overcome them.

- **Talk About It:** Share your feelings with a trusted friend, mentor, or fellow artist. When you feel down or your self-doubts start to creep in, talk it out with someone and get it out of your system. Opening up can provide relief and valuable perspective.

- **Track and Challenge Negative Thoughts:** We cannot really control our minds and change the way we think instantly. It is a process. Keep a journal to document instances of imposter feelings. Challenge these thoughts by presenting evidence of your achievements and capabilities. Focus on those instead of the negative feelings. Distract your negative thoughts and divert them towards more positive ones. With evidence, it will be easier for you to believe that you can do it.

- **Celebrate Small Wins:** Acknowledge and celebrate your accomplishments, no matter how small. Because every step you take towards becoming a better version of yourself, away from self-doubt, is a step in the right direction. Each step forward is a triumph against imposter syndrome.

- **Embrace Continuous Learning:** Shift your focus from being perfect to being a continuous learner. The world is constantly changing, and new technology, techniques, etc. are being introduced every day. One cannot simply know it all. Be open to learning something new whenever you can. Be open to upgrading yourself at every chance you get. It may be in terms of your style, technique, medium, or anything else. Embrace growth and improvement rather than perfection.

Cultivating Resilience: Building a Stronger Artistic Self

By consistently practicing these strategies, you cultivate resilience against Imposter Syndrome. When you do so, you automatically start propelling towards a more positive way of thinking. This is rather beneficial for your self-growth. Remember, overcoming this battle is not a one-time victory but a journey of self-acceptance, growth, and triumph over self-doubt. So please be kind to yourself.

Your authentic artistic journey awaits.

By conquering imposter syndrome, you free yourself to fully embrace your artistic identity. Recognise that every artist faces this formidable foe, but it is your determination and resilience that will shape your path towards an authentic and flourishing artistic career. The canvas of your destiny is yours to paint—bold, confident, and imposter-free. Close your eyes and imagine yourself there! It's beautiful, isn't it?

Loaded with all the knowledge about what has been stopping you, we will do another simple but enriching exercise.

The Self – Appreciation Canvas

Here is what you need to do.

Gather your supplies.
A blank sheet of paper or a sketchbook.
Pens, coloured pencils, or markers.
Go to a place where you love to create. It can be your desk, a favourite nook in your house, or anywhere. You can probably help yourself to a mug of coffee, hot chocolate, or a cup of tea. Maybe play some of your favourite music that you like listening to while you create. Make yourself comfortable.

Create a visualisation.
Close your eyes for a moment and visualise a canvas filled with positivity, admiration, and self-love. Picture it as vibrant, energising, and tailored just for you.

List your achievements.
On the sheet of paper, jot down at least five achievements you are proud of in your artistic journey. These could be big or small, personal or professional.

Express your strengths.
Next, write down three artistic strengths or skills you possess that you deeply appreciate about yourself. It could be anything from your ability to capture emotions in your work, your unique style, or your dedication to improving.

Doodle Your Joy:

Let your creative side shine. Surround your achievements and strengths with doodles, drawings, or designs that make you feel joyful and empowered. This is your canvas, and you have all the freedom to do what pleases you. Let yourself loose and just create!

Add positive affirmations:

Write positive affirmations that resonate with you. For instance, "I am a talented and unique artist," "My art brings joy and inspiration to others," or "I am capable of achieving my artistic dreams."

Display your creation:

Hang this self-appreciation canvas in your workspace or any place you'll see it frequently. Let it remind you of your achievements, strengths, and the positive energy within you. So at any moment, you find your thoughts slowly crawling towards our foe, the imposter syndrome, take a look at your 'Self Appreciation Canvas'. Reset your mind and reaffirm to yourself that you are awesome, just the way you are!

Go ahead, look at this wonderful self-appreciation canvas you have created for yourself as many times as you can, and constantly remind yourself that you are amazing.

The Yellow Door,
by Crazy R.

Heartbreaks are like life's remarkable tutors, aren't they? At 26 and 27, they were pivotal in polishing my artistry. Speaking of influences, there is another person I would like to mention, a college mate, Sanjay. He is an incredible artist with a bit of a controversial aura around him. A guy with the heart of a kid but a don's face.

Sanjay saw my art during this time while I was also applying to The Bauhaus School of Art. I have always dreamt of studying art abroad, but that dream has not materialised yet. However, this dream of mine seems to be taking on a different shape. Instead, I found myself creating my own school.

Bauhaus was a moment in Germany when people started transitioning more towards an angular style of architecture. It has had a significant influence on the current style of modern architecture. It was less decorative and more focused on straight lines, geometric shapes, and simplified designs. And this obviously found its way into art. Bauhaus School of Art gave me an assignment as part of the enrollment process. They wanted me to create art for the public. As an architect, I believe art should be for everyone, not just the rich. So, I took up the challenge of making art that everyone could enjoy.

I did not have much money, barely 2,000 rupees ($25) left in my account each month. But I was determined to make this happen. Amid my daily routine and earning a living, I came up with a plan. I decided to place a bright yellow door in the busiest part of my town. You might wonder, Why a door?

I decided to place a yellow door in a public area. Even though it was initially for a school project, I wanted to make it a big deal. I had some followers on Instagram and locals interested in what I was doing, so I decided to invite them to join in.

To build excitement, I posted about painting on the streets and invited people to watch. I made a plan by gathering pictures from Pinterest and imagining what I wanted to do, although I had no clue how to make it happen. I started creating hype on Instagram, counting down the days until this event.

I said I was going to be painting on the streets and welcomed everyone to join me and watch it. I chose a special location: a bridge connecting the old and new parts of town, because it symbolised connections and contrasts in life, like good and bad, old and new. This bridge was a part of my canvas. I called it the *"Door of Duality"* I just wanted people to come and experience something new. It was a free art show, and I wanted to see how people would react to the door.

I did jugaad (a non-conventional hack) to get a scrap door from a market with half of my last two thousand rupees. I rented a truck for the rest of the thousand rupees ($12) to transport the door. After getting permission from the authorities, I took the door to the bridge and placed it there. It was a yellow door—I just had a thing for that colour back then. I closed it and watched it for two days, and soon the whole town was buzzing with curiosity.

Around twenty-five thousand people saw it, and it went viral on social media. I had a friend in the media, and I asked him to share this crazy thing I was doing if he found it interesting. The response was wild! Thirteen thousand people saw the door on the first day alone.

The second day was even more exciting. I started painting on the door, and that was when it really caught the attention of many more. People began talking about this bold artist painting on the streets. It turned into a social experiment of sorts.

I painted an eye on the door, a symbol of perspective. I wanted to convey that that is how we see ourselves and life. Sometimes opportunities are right in front of us, but we fail to see or seize them, like this book is right in front of you to start your art business. But will you take the opportunity? The door represented possibilities in life, sometimes wide open, sometimes seemingly locked.

As I painted that eye and metaphorically opened the door, something amazing happened. A child passing by crossed through the door. It was incredible to see how their curiosity led them to explore what was beyond that door. Kids, with their endless curiosity, teach us so much.

While many were curious or sceptical about my public stunt, there was this one child intrigued by the colourful door. This small act by the child inspired others from various walks of life—joggers, couples, the elderly, rich, and poor—to walk through the door. People started crossing from the old city to the new city, and vice versa. It was a clear indication that art truly belongs to everyone.

I was capturing these moments from a hidden spot and received help from photographers and the media. I even wrote a blog about the whole experiment and its purpose. This initiative inspired writers and people to express themselves. They saw it as a unique concept, and suddenly, there was talk about this mysterious artist named Crazy R.

I was soon motivated to paint more. I wanted to paint a series. So I did just that. It started with the idea of a child's transformation in the mother's womb—the first painting depicted this. The second one portrayed my playground memories, where I found a sense of home in the joy of playing on lush green grass. As a teenager, my idea of home shifted to endless tuition and IIT classes, emphasising the academic pursuit. Then, when I travelled extensively, I discovered a new concept of home. Every stranger I met offered support and kindness, giving me a sense of family and love I had always sought. This marked a transition in my idea of home.

This particular series was titled "Man of No Ego." It was about shedding the ego that often builds up as we acquire numerous titles and roles in life— architect, interior designer, mother, sister, among others. With time, these roles sometimes make us crave respect, love, and wealth, leading to an inflated ego.

To address this, I created colourful paintings

representing various emotions. However, within these vibrant colours, I incorporated a dark element, symbolising the ego. Each painting had dripping paint reaching the ground, symbolising the melting away of the ego.

This series was special to me. I sold three or four of these paintings, but they remain close to my heart. The movement and the way these artworks came to life were truly enjoyable. It was a collection of ten paintings called "Man of No Ego," which taught me valuable lessons along the way. It is always good to work on a series. Because you can tell a story through them.

If you wish to learn to come up with the concepts and ideas to create ten or twenty paintings on a concept, we do an annual retreat every year in some beautiful location, which is called the FAT Art Business Retreat. This will help you get to work and create an idea of what paintings you want to do for your next solo show.

There was a turning point when I realised the sheer power of social media. I realised I had potential buyers, a network, access to cafes and spaces for workshops, and a student base willing to invest in my offerings. Establishing my brand demanded skills that required consistent honing. Even now, I strive daily to perfect these abilities, aiming to become a master in my craft.

I have come to realise that the three most lucrative skills globally are

- Sales,
- Marketing through social media, and
- Copywriting.

Master these, and you will never face financial woes. Amidst managing various income streams, I prioritised refining my sales and marketing skills. Yet, as an artist, there are more essential skills to grasp for a successful journey. Allow me to guide you through the smart skills you need to become a skilled 'smartpreneur' in the art world.

Read on to learn some of the smart skills that are essential for your art business journey.

Smart Skills

Artistic skills.

An artist is someone who creates art. So this has to be the strongest skill set you must possess as an artist. Just like in any other field where people study further to upgrade themselves professionally, you, as an artist, have to always look for ways and means to grow your skills.
Let us look at a set of artistic skills that you can focus on.

Drawing in Sketching:
Drawing and sketching are the foundations of any artist. You have to be able to draw or sketch your subject, whatever it may be. You have to be able to transfer what you see in your mind onto a surface for other people to be able to see it too. So,

mastering your fundamental drawing and sketching techniques is foundational for creating artwork across various mediums.

Colour theory and mixing

Colours add life to everything around us. Colours speak to our emotions. They have a mental and emotional effect on us. We react differently to different colours. For instance, cooler colours have a calming effect on us, whereas warmer colours have the exact opposite effect on us. For example, restaurants and food-related designs are advised to have more red because people feel hungry when they look at the colour. This is known as colour psychology. The basics for this are to understand colour theory and how colours work. Learning this at the very beginning will help you go a long way in your art journey.

Colour theory is where you learn the art of mixing various colours to get more colours and what colours go well together and what do not. Therefore, understanding colour theory, colour harmony, and effective colour mixing are essential for creating visually and emotionally appealing artwork.

Composition and Design:

Now we all know that there is no such thing as a good design or a bad design. It is only the different perspectives that people have. However, no matter the style of art, the medium used, or the idea behind it, certain fundamentals of composition and design naturally work well. They are aesthetically pleasing to look at. And every appealing art piece has good composition and design. It is about how the colours and elements in your art are composed. Learning the principles of composition and design helps in arranging the elements within the artwork in such a way that you get maximum impact and balance as a viewer. And that is what successful artwork has to have.

Perspective and proportions:
Perspectives give you a sense of depth. Proportions give you a sense of scale. Understanding these two factors and applying them to your artwork will add that extra aspect of realism or surrealism to your art. With that, you can communicate so much of what you visualise in your mind. If you, as an artist, are visualising a certain object of a certain size from a certain height and distance, it is understanding how to apply perspectives and proportions that will help you transfer the same on your canvas. It helps you show depth and dimension in your artwork.

Understanding light and shadow:
Every surface, unless it is completely black reflects or refracts light. It is light and shadow that lets us see things. Otherwise, it will all just look flat. If you wish to add that touch of realism and depth to your

artwork, you must learn how light and shadow work.

Painting Technique:
There are many different mediums of paint. There are many different techniques to paint using each medium. And being proficient in your medium, may it be oils, acrylics, watercolours, or even digital is very important for you as an artist. You need to know your medium and keep looking for ways and means to learn as much as you can about it.

Sculpting and modelling:
Sculpting and modelling are something that you can practise and learn if you wish to become a sculptor. Clay sculptors and items and accessories are also quite popular these days and have quite a cast customer base. If you focus on building your skills and developing your own style, you will attract your own set of customers. In order to become proficient in sculpting and modelling, you need to learn about the various materials, and how form and structure work.

Printmaking:
When you create one piece and sell it, it is a rare item, and yes, it will be one of a kind. However, you can make multiple copies of your artwork and sell it to many more people for a slightly lesser cost, but still make more than what you would make if

you sold just one piece. Besides, with printmaking, you can also transfer your artwork onto many other surfaces, which will make it more versatile and more widely available, thereby reaching a wider audience. Some of the printmaking techniques are etching, Art lithography, and silk screening.

2. Digital Skills

Graphic Design:
Graphic design has seen a huge boom in the art industry. So learning the right software for creating digital artwork, logos, and promotional materials like Adobe Illustrator, Coral Draw, etc. is what will help you as a graphic designer.

Digital painting and digital illustration:
With digital painting and illustration software like Adobe Photoshop, Adobe Illustrator, Procreate, Corel Painter, and similar tools, you can create digital art that can be used in so many different ways, from book designing to posters to merchandise. Mastering these tools is definitely required for any digital artist.

3D modelling and animation:
3D animation is a whole different world of opportunities on its own. If you are looking to become a 3D animation artist, and software like Blender, Maya, or Z Brush can be good ones to

explore, learn, and master.

Video and multimedia editing:

No matter what form of art you wish to create, videos are a brilliant way to connect with your audience. Instagram reels and YouTube shorts are good ways to upload short videos that last only a few seconds but can grab the attention of many people. Not only shorts, but you can also upload art tutorials and make them more entertaining and informative by inserting supportive elements like clipart, text, music, and even voiceovers. In order to do this, you need to learn to edit your videos and multimedia content. You can look into software like Adobe Premiere Pro, Inshots, You Cut, or Final Cut Pro to showcase your art, tutorials, vlogs, or even advertise your art.

3. Business Marketing Skills:

Entrepreneurship and Business Acumen:

Now that you have the mindset and have started to get better at your art skills, another area that needs attention from you is your business and how you do it. There are certain business skills that you will have to acquire if you have not already, and you should keep developing them. Knowledge of business principles, financial management, and entrepreneurship to run an art business effectively is a given requirement. Because you cannot only focus on your art. You also need to become a businessperson and think like one. Effective financial management is a crucial skill you have to develop early on in your business for you to be able to keep your business afloat no matter what.

Marketing and branding:
It is not enough if you just know how to create art and start a business. A business is successful only once you put it out there and start making money. For that to happen, you need to let your audience know what you are doing. And for that to happen, you need to market your business. You need to create a brand for yourself. That way, you can effectively present and promote artwork to a target audience.

Networking and relationship building:
Being a part of a community can be beneficial to you in more ways than you can imagine. You can meet fellow artists, get exposed to newer ideas, and gain more visibility to establish and maintain relationships with fellow artists, galleries, clients, and art enthusiasts.

Being a part of a community can be beneficial to you in more ways than you can imagine. By communicating with more like-minded people and fellow artists, you will get more exposure. You will get to understand what the art world is like on a larger scale. You need to know how to build relationships with fellow artists, art galleries, clients, and art enthusiasts because it is a skill in itself. Knowledge of how to network, find and meet people, and maintain those relationships is instrumental because they will guide you and be there for you in the long run, and you can do the same for them.

Negotiation and sales:
As an art business person, it is not enough for you to just know how to create art or how to start a business. You also need to know how to be smart with your expenses and your money. You must know how to negotiate when you make purchases and sales with your vendors and potential buyers. So you have to learn to develop your negotiating skills to get better prices in your sales as well as effectively communicate with your potential buyers.

4. Personal development skills:

Time management and organisation:
Among the many skills that you have to learn as an art business person, organising your time and managing it effectively is essential because you have to create art, market it, take care of all the administrative tasks, and focus on your personal life. None of these is less important than the other, and you have to be able to manage them well to be able to have a good balance in your life.

Adaptability and flexibility:

The world is changing every day. There is new software, new technology, new art forms, and so much more. Something new is introduced to us on a daily basis, and the styles are ever-changing. You have to be able to accept those changes and learn to adapt to the changing trends. Technology and market demands in the art world for you to keep growing as a businessperson and as an artist and be successful in the same.

Resilience and perseverance:

Just like in life, businesses, no matter what kind, will have ups and downs. You need to know that no failure is bad and that everything is just another opportunity for us to learn and become better at what we are doing. You have to learn to have the capacity to bounce back from setbacks, rejections, and challenges and continue pursuing your artistic goals. Because with every challenge and mistake you make, you are going to take a lesson from it that you will carry for life. It is only going to take you a step closer to your success.

Self-motivation and discipline:

If you were an office worker, you would have had a routine and stuck to it. However, when you are an artist and you have a business of your own, it is a lot more challenging for you to be able to stick to a schedule and follow it on a daily basis. Try to follow a routine from the very beginning of your art business journey. Because it is very easy to go off track, let yourself get into that slump, and let lethargy take over. You need to have self-motivation and learn to be disciplined with your time and routine.

Critical thinking and problem-solving:
Businesses always throw challenges at us, and we have to have a positive attitude towards approaching those challenges instead of letting them bog us down. You need to be able to look at these challenges creatively and effectively and work towards solving them instead of giving up.

Emotional intelligence:
The reason any art becomes special is because the viewers are able to connect to the art in a very deep emotional sense. It can be any kind of emotion, but it has to have the ability to evoke those emotions in a person, and the only way your art can do that is if you are aware of how emotions work and understand other people's emotions. You need to know how to manage these emotions and use this understanding in your artistic expression and interactions with them. You can come across as being more heartfelt and genuine to your buyer or anyone who views your art.

Continuous learning and curiosity:
One of the best ways to keep your passion and interest alive and not get distracted is to stay

curious. We all know how children are bold in exploring the world around them and are more creative. That is because they are curious about the world around them. You have to bring out that inner child, entertain that curiosity of yours, and continue to seek new inspirations and techniques to grow as an artist.

Digital art tools proficiency:
Digital art has become such a huge part of the art industry in recent years, and learning how to work with the necessary tools and software is foundational. Especially if you are a digital artist, you have to try and learn and educate yourself as much as you can about platforms like Adobe Creative Suite, Procreate, and Corel Draw because these are essential for creating and enhancing digital artwork.

Why is it important?
Just like a traditional artist, for example, a watercolour artist has to know how the brushes, the canvas, and the techniques that go into creating the artwork work, as a digital artist, you have to know how your digital tools work, and these significantly enhance your capabilities as an artist, allowing you to acquire more precise and detailed results. Experiment more and be more efficient in your workflow in the digital domain.

Online portfolio curation:

As an artist, your portfolio is like your CV. It is a little bit more than your CV because it is going to communicate to your clients what you do. More often than not, it could be how your client or your end buyer is going to have that first impression of you and your artwork. So your portfolio has to speak for you. It has to reflect who you are and what your art is. So creating and maintaining an appealing online portfolio that showcases a diverse range of your artwork and effectively presenting the same in your own unique style plays a very important role in what the client is going to think of you.

Why is it important?

Your online portfolio acts as your digital storefront. It is more like your display. If you had a physical store, you would display the best of your products, which would attract customers. Similarly, your portfolio acts as your digital shop display. It will help you attract potential clients, collaborators, and opportunities.

Social media marketing:

Social media is one of the biggest contributors to connecting your art to your audience and potential buyers. Social media has such an important role to play in your artistic journey. And so, understanding social media platforms and the strategies that they use effectively will help you promote your artwork, engage with the audience, and build a community of followers.

Why is it important?
Social media is such a powerful tool for visibility, connecting with a global audience, and marketing artwork directly to potential buyers without having to go through middlemen or art galleries. People get to know who you are as a person, and you are able to connect better that way. This, in turn, increases the possibility of them wanting to buy your products.

8. E-commerce in Online Sales Skills:
Gone are the days when one had to go to a physical store to buy any product. This is the digital age where everything can be done online, and e-commerce platforms rule. In this digital age, everything from buying products to making payments can be done online. So you need to have a thorough knowledge of how e-commerce platforms and payment gateways work. This, along with effective online sales strategies and understanding e-commerce trends and customer behaviour, can help you build a very successful art business that gives you a constant source of income.

Why is it important?
When you have a physical store, your reach and potential customers are very limited. However,

when you sell your artwork online, the kind of reach it has on a global scale is unbelievable compared to the former. Selling your artwork online expands your market reach it enables you to directly sell to a diverse and even international clientele. This can literally help you put your artwork out there in the world.

9. Digital photography and image editing:

In today's world, with social media and e-commerce playing such a huge role in any kind of business, you have to be able to present your artwork to your audience, no matter where they are from, in such a way that when they see it, they know almost exactly what it looks like when they see it in person. Therefore, you need to know how to capture high-quality images of your artwork and use image editing software to enhance and optimise your images to be able to display them online. Low-quality images or pictures that do not really bring out the beauty of your art will not appeal to your customers, so you have to be able to aesthetically present it to them.

Why is it important?

It helps you enhance the online visibility of your business. It helps increase the possibility of attracting a broader audience and potential buyers.

10. Basic coding and web design

As intimidating as it may sound if you are not an IT

person, it is not that scary. There are a lot of tools that are now available for you to be able to easily create websites. Familiarity with HTML, CSS, and web design principles helps you manage and customise your artist's website and portfolio. You also have platforms like Wix where you can design and build your entire website for free. You can acquire extra features for a small fee. It will make running your business a lot easier.

Why is it important?
Basic coding skills allow you to personalise your online presence, providing a unique and tailored experience for your visitors.

11. Collaboration and networking:
When you collaborate with other artists, designers, professionals, or businesses, your opportunities only increase because you are able to reach their customer base as well. Collaborating with like-minded people gives you more possibilities to grow your audience, who have similar tastes. This helps you leverage networking opportunities in the digital space.

Why is it important?
Collaboration and networking can lead to joint projects, exposure to new markets, and increased visibility within the artistic community.

12. Data analytics and insight interpretation

With online platforms playing such an important role in your art business, it is important for you to know how to analyse the data and interpret the same. With this information, you can adapt strategies and make informed decisions.

For example, you may have noticed that reels on Instagram do better than photos, and those reels, when posted at a certain time, on a certain day, seem to have a larger reach than when posted at a different time (when it is not one of the peak hours). Most social media platforms offer insights so you can have an almost clear idea as to how your post is performing. It can be as detailed as where your audience is from, what the majority age group is, and what the peak hours of traffic for your page are. Depending on this information you can decide what kind of posts you can go ahead with to increase engagement in your account.

Why is it important?

Data-driven decisions can optimise market efforts. It can help you identify your target audience and refine your online strategies to get better results.

13. Cyber security awareness:

With so much of your data online, it is also exposed to as much potential online risks. Therefore you have to be aware of online security, privacy, and protection and learn to take the necessary measures to safeguard your digital assets, customer data, and online transactions.

Why is it important?

 With every day that goes by the dependence on digital media increases and you need to protect you need to protect your work and personal information from potential cyber threats. There is a lot of information that you are putting out there that belongs to you as well as your clients. You have to be careful and safeguard the same.

Before we proceed further with my story, let me share how you can acquire all those skills that we just saw and become a successful artist. Hold my hand. As the slope gets steeper, we might have to take more steps. Attaining these skills can take a while and requires a lot of dedication from you. Skills take time to acquire. but if the foundations are right, the building is stronger. So as an artist, just your art skills are not enough; you need these additional skills to make money. The slope can be steep, but your willpower should be strong.

Ways to acquire smart skills

Let us dive into the various ways you can acquire all the smart skills that we discussed previously.

Art school or university:
There are a lot of art schools and universities that offer specialised courses in different forms of art and mediums, and you can choose from them. You can decide based on what you wish to study and improve your skills on. Consider enrolling in a reputable art school or university that offers a variety of programmes related to fine arts, graphic design, illustration, culture, or any specific art or discipline you are interested in.
Do your research and choose a programme that aligns with your artistic goals and desired skill set.

Online courses in workshops:

Platforms and websites:
There are a number of online platforms like Coursera, Udemy, Skillshare, Khan Academy, Domestika, and LinkedIn Learning that offer a wide range of courses in art, design, and related subjects. You do not have to physically attend the university if you cannot. You can do it online by sitting at home or on the go. Most of them also offer free courses.

Choose courses that focus on your areas of interest, whether it is drawing, painting, digital art, or business skills that can include photography, marketing, and financial management.

Art workshops and seminars:
Local art centres and events:
With a little bit of research on what is happening around you, you will find many workshops, seminars, and art events that could be happening in your city. They may be conducted by local art centres, galleries, or artists. So look around your own city and explore.

Participate in live workshops, learn new techniques, and gain insights. Connect with new people, build your skill set, and grow.

Self-directed learning:
Books and publications:
Another way you can learn something new is by reading art-related books, journals, and magazines that cover techniques, theory, art history, other businesses, and even stories and interviews of artists or designers. You might pick something from them.

Choose books written by well-known authors who are also subject-matter experts. So you get the best out of the best.

Online tutorials and blogs:
Another way to learn something by yourself is by exploring online art tutorials and blogs that are mostly available for free on various platforms, like the ones mentioned above or even YouTube. They cover a wide range of artistic skills and topics. You can view the art processes that artists have uploaded. There are people who upload free tutorials online for you to just watch and learn, or with which you can paint or create along with them. It is a world full of possibilities, so you do not have to worry about having to enrol in a specific university just to be able to develop the skills.

Mentorship and guidance:
Seek a mentor:
It always helps to have someone to guide you on your journey. Looking for a mentor or an

experienced artist who is willing to teach and provide you with valuable feedback on your artwork is priceless. You are not just reading it out of a book or watching a video; you are actually having a one-on-one interaction with someone who has already mastered the skills and has had experience. Nothing can beat the lessons learned from experience, whether in life or in business. You will definitely gain so much more knowledge when you get to meet a mentor.

Engage in regular discussions and critiques to enhance your skills and knowledge.

Networking and collaboration:
Art communities:
Join art communities, online and offline, to connect with solo artists, share experiences, and collaborate on projects. Remember, collaboration is always better than competition.

Engage in discussions, attend art meet-ups, and actively participate in community events.

Practice and experimentation:
Regular practice:
Practice always leads to improvement. You have to consistently practice to consistently grow. In your routine, schedule a certain amount of time regularly to practice and experiment with various artistic techniques and mediums.

Set achievable goals and challenge yourself to art. challenges so you can improve continuously. You can also take up an art challenge, wherein you challenge yourself to a specific stretch of time, like 15 days or 21 days, and work on your art. At the end of this challenge, you will be able to see a considerable difference and improvement between your first day and your twenty-first day. This can also boost your self-confidence and give you self-motivation. You will develop the habit of being consistent with your art practice.

Personal projects:

Apart from working on commissions that you receive from clients, you will also have to set aside some time to work on your personal art projects that align with your artistic vision and interests. In doing so, you will be able to build your technique, experiment more, explore more, and grow as an artist. So you will be your client and create what you really want to create. You can experiment and do something different. Experiment with different styles, themes, and concepts to broaden your creative horizons. Because there is no one to control you or tell you what you need to do, and you are free to explore what you wish on your canvas.

Internships and real-world experience:
Art studios and galleries:
It is one thing to learn from books, videos, and theory, but it is an entirely different experience to explore opportunities and experience the same. Try to work at an art studio, a gallery, or with a creative agency because it helps you gain hands-on experience and insight into how the art industry functions. You will get the inside scoop. This can be very important and useful in your journey as an art businessperson.

In doing so, you also get to learn about the business side of art, customer interactions, and exhibitions. You get exposure to what is trending. You can learn how to approach people and how people approach artists.

Feedback and critique:
Peer reviews:
Do not hesitate to seek feedback from fellow artists, mentors, and other online art communities to understand areas for improvement and gain diverse perspectives. Take suggestions as constructive criticism and work on how you can improve. Apply these suggestions and see how they work with your art.

Attend art exhibitions and events:
Local exhibitions:
You can also attend art exhibitions, gallery

openings, and art fairs in your locality or nearby cities that showcase works by different artists.

In doing so, you get to observe different styles and techniques and interact with art enthusiasts to expand your understanding of the art world.

Stay up-to-date with trends:
Follow industry trends:
It is always important to stay informed and updated about the latest trends, techniques, and emerging technologies in the industry that you belong to, and the art industry is no exception.

One way to do so is to follow art influencers, industry bloggers, and relevant social media accounts to stay updated.

Financial management and business skills:
Financial literacy:
One of the ways to manage your finances. when you are running your art business is to take a basic financial literacy course to understand budgeting, managing income, pricing strategies, and financial planning for your art business.

With these skills, you will definitely be fully equipped to face any challenges that come your way in your art business journey. These are what make you a Smartpreneur.

2020, The Pandemic

Coming back to my story, after acquiring various skills and serving diverse clients, my income remained inconsistent. Sometimes I made a lot, while other times I made barely enough to get by. I was making 10,000, 20,000, or 30,000 rupees ($360). This inconsistency troubled me deeply. I had become overly reliant on my art business, and despite everything, it seemed like I had nothing.

There were earlier dreams, too. Initially, I aspired to be a
pilot, but the Indian Air Force's requirement for unmarried males prevented me from pursuing that path back in 2016. That was dream crash number one. Then came the dream of attending SAIC in Chicago (I will be sharing a little more about it shortly), followed by the upheaval caused by COVID—dream crash number three.

In 2020, the pandemic hit. COVID-19 brought the world to a standstill, and my business suffered the same fate. I could not go out or work on my projects. Being someone who loved travelling and exploring suddenly facing these limitations felt like abruptly stopping while climbing a mountain, which was quite a shock.

It became a significant turning point for me. Initially, I had big plans for 2020. I had booked flights to Dubai to take my art journey to the next level by participating in the World Art Dubai Festival. But then the world came to a standstill due to the pandemic, and my dream of attending that festival was shattered.

Everyone went indoors, and with the isolation came stress, depression, and anxiety. While I continued painting daily, it was productive creatively, but financially, it was challenging. I learned that, as an artist, recognition with money holds greater significance than mere appreciation. The need for financial acknowledgement had become ingrained in me, and I had some money left from all the work I had done until then.

With only around two lakh rupees left, I needed a sustainable solution. I began researching ways to monetize my art online. That's when I stumbled upon print-on-demand services, NFTs (non-fungible tokens), and other online avenues for income. This exploration marked the beginning of my journey to explore online methods of monetizing my art.

It was quite a challenging phase. Despite seven months of intense online research, I couldn't find a sustainable source of income. I tried various avenues, from exploring e-commerce to setting up an Etsy shop, but everything required more energy and in-depth research. It became overwhelming, and I felt drained trying to find the right online income source.

Feeling disheartened by the lack of results, I was on the verge of giving up. That's when I started helping a friend with branding for their industry or company. It was a fresh challenge, introducing me to a new skill set and a different problem to solve.

Through this experience, I realised that branding was a skill I excelled at. I had a knack for positioning and creating brands that could thrive in any business. It became apparent that I possessed unique skills in assisting businesses, encompassing sales, marketing, and branding strategies.

Great! We are almost there! But there is yet another very important chapter we will have to discuss in your journey as a smartpreneur, and that is branding. We will look into the depths of how smart branding works and uncover its potential to transform you from being an aspiring artist to building your own artistic empire.

The Power of Smart Branding

Introduction to the Power of Smart Branding:

In the ever-growing and ever-competitive art world where creativity meets commerce, branding is a very powerful tool that can

- Elevate an artist's profile,
- Impact the influence the artist has,
- Impact the perceptions people will have of the artist
- And can help the artist carve a niche in the hearts of their audience

Smart branding is not just about a logo or a tagline. It is a strategic combination of art, storytelling values, and perception management.

The Art of Branding:
Definition:
'Branding is the promotion of a particular product accompanied by means of advertising and distinctive design'.

Branding is more than just your visual identity. It includes both the emotional connection and perceptions that you have with people and that people have of you. It is how people associate it with who you are. It is about crafting a unique identity that sets you apart in the art world.

In the art industry, branding plays a huge role because it represents you. It has to represent what you give to your audience in the form of your artwork. When you understand the true essence of branding, it empowers you, as an artist, to strategically position yourself and your work. It communicates the value of what you do to your end buyers.

The Brand Identity:
When you think about your brand, ask yourself: What does your brand consist of? What is your brand identity? What are the things that go into your brand identity? Let us look at it a bit more in detail. When we talk about brand identity, it includes the visual elements like the logo and colour schemes and the intangible aspects of the brand like your brand voice and values. It emphasises the importance of a cohesive brand identity that mirrors the artist's essence and resonates with the audience. So it has to be able to communicate with them without you speaking.

When you establish a strong brand identity, it

enables you to create a lasting and memorable impression on your audience, and they are then able to recognise and connect with your work a lot more easily.

Crafting your brand story:
The Power of Narrative:

As kids, we were more drawn to stories, and as people, we get to connect better with people whom we share experiences with. When you tell your audience a compelling story about your journey, through your brand, and the struggles you had to face when you chose to become an artist, when you talk about what inspired you and about your passion, you can evoke some very strong emotions in people and forge a deeper connection with your audience.

When your brand story is well crafted, it helps you humanise your brand, making it relatable and inspiring. It ultimately captures the hearts and minds of your audience.

Aligning with your artistic journey

One way to tell a compelling story is to intertwine your personal experiences, growth, and evolution as an artist into your brand story. You can combine some experiences that you had in your life as you embarked on this journey as an artist and bring them into your brand story. You can share how it helps you or contributes to building your brand.

When you do this, you see that the story behind your brand is a lot more authentic, and people like authenticity. This helps you form a strong emotional connection with your audience.

Building a digital brand presence:
Website and Portfolio:
When you create art and you have your business plan, the next step for you to take is to have a platform where, when they look at it, they have to know that this is who you are and what you do. As mentioned earlier, your portfolio oftentimes becomes your first point of contact, the first way your customer or potential buyer develops a first impression of you and your work. So creating these two mindfully is of utmost importance. It has to be aesthetically pleasing. It has to be functional, effectively show your work, and represent the visual identity of your brand. You cannot have a website that is hard to navigate where people who visit it feel confused as to where they should look for what they need.

Providing a well-designed website acts as a good digital home for your brand and a space for you to exhibit your work, share your background story, and leave a lasting impression on your visitors. They must want to come back for more.

Social media mastery:
I cannot insist more on the importance of the role

of social media platforms as an essential tool for building your digital brand presence. When you strategize and plan your posts and your presence on your social media platforms, it is a definite step towards success. You have to be able to use them for your benefit.

Social media helps you reach a broader audience and directly interact with your followers. This helps you establish genuine one-on-one communication and engagement with your following, thereby creating a mark for your brand in the digital landscape.

Navigating the visual language of branding:
When we create a brand design or logo, there are a lot of things that come into play. It is not just a logo. It is not just your website; it is a combination of everything.

Colour psychology:
Colours have an effect on people. We, as humans, have a psychological reaction to the colours around us. Just like how blue is calming, red is related to passion, and yellow is cheerful, every colour has a psychological reaction on us. They influence human emotions and perceptions. So when you design your brand's visual appearance, you have to focus on what kind of colour palette you use. It has to align with your brand personality, and it has to effectively communicate the message

that your brand has for your audience.

So when you do in-depth research on colour psychology, it helps you as an artist to strategically use the colours in your branding to evoke certain emotions and create a memorable brand image.

Typography and visual elements:
Now that you have decided on what your brand story is and what colour you are going to be using to represent your brand, you will next have to look at the kind of typography that you will be using.

For example, if you had a name for your brand and a logo, there would be a certain font that you might want to use. It has to be something that you relate to. Some people may like floral fonts, and some people may like a more stylized font, and some may like something more formal. Whatever it is that you can really connect with, that is what you must choose.

Let us say that you are a watercolour artist and your brand's typography has a brush stroke-styled font. Then anyone who looks at your brand can tell that what you do is related to painting.

So when you clearly understand typography and the visual elements that go along with it, it ensures that your brand's visual communication is cohesive and resonates with the intended message that you would like to convey through your brand design. You have to focus on visual communication because people tend to retain things that they visually look at in their memory.

Connecting with your audience:
Target audience analysis:
When you sell a product, you have a certain target audience in mind that you are making it for. If you were to make framed artwork, it would probably be for people who might want to gift your famed artwork to their loved ones or for interior designers and architects who would like to deck up homes that they design with your artwork.

So you will have to do comprehensive research to identify and understand your target audience. Your brand message needs to be tailored for them. You have to meet the specific preferences and expectations of your target audience by approaching them in an artistic manner, and you should also understand where your target audience is from because demographics matter too.

When you understand your target audience, it helps in creating content that can directly resonate with the right kind of people that you wish to communicate with and reach out to. Your artwork becomes a lot more relatable because, when they see it, they know it is something that is made for them. This enhances engagement and increases brand loyalty.

Engagement strategies:
As people, we like communication, and your audience is no different. They like it when they are being communicated to. Any kind of engagement strategy to effectively connect with your audience is always effective. You have to create interactive content where their opinions are also taken into account, and that way they know that their opinions matter. When you apply those opinions to your artwork, it has an extra touch of customer service.

Your audience will be happy. How do you get them to engage? Here are ways you can include them in your business:
- Create interactive content,
- Respond to comments and messages.
- Have contests; get them to participate in them and
- Foster a sense of community among your followers.

Implementing these strategies would go a long way towards retaining loyal customers who want to come back to you for more. Because when you do this, it becomes a lot more than just the product that you are giving them; it becomes an experience. Doing so not only builds a loyal fan base, but it also provides valuable feedback and insights to refine your brand's approach. When you have repeat customers, you know that they know your brand, and any suggestions they make will only help you better your brand, and you can apply those suggestions to your products.

Authenticity and brand integrity:
Authenticity in branding:
You cannot go wrong with authenticity. It is very important for you to be authentic when you put your brand out there. This will also help you have a consistent brand image that aligns with your values. Your values, your beliefs, and your artistic style have to be genuine, and anyone would appreciate authenticity.

It builds trust and credibility. These are two of the most essential factors that influence how the audience receives and connects with your brand. Because when people feel you are trustworthy, nothing can go wrong, and you have to make sure that you keep the trust going by only giving them genuine, good-quality products in return. Why would anyone say no to something genuine, right?

Brand consistency:
When you have a brand that you have designed around a certain style or a message, for example, if you have a brand that advocates eco-friendly products, then you have to have that message resonating everywhere in your brand. It has to be

seen everywhere—in your products, your packaging, your advertising, and everywhere you can think of. That way, you convey your message strongly, and there is consistency that is maintained across your brand. So when someone looks at anything related to your brand, they will know that this is what you stand for, this is what you believe in, and this is what your brand encourages. It reinforces your brand identity and message in a coherent and recognisable manner.

When your brand consistency is maintained, your audience will have a unified and memorable experience, which enhances brand recall and trust. Going back to our example, you consistently maintained the idea of sustainable living throughout everything in your product branding. Anything sustainable will remind your customers of your brand. That is how you encourage that sense of brand recall and trust through your branding.

Collaborations and Partnerships:
Strategic alliances:
The idea of having a strategic alliance and partnership in the art world is to encourage working together and expanding together. Collaborative efforts with other artists and organisations of brands can increase the reach and influence you have on people because when you collaborate with another artist, your work is being

exposed to their followers and audience, and their work is being exposed to your followers and your audience. Thereby, it becomes a larger community. Similarly, by collaborating with large organisations or brands, your reach is a lot wider.

Another way to go about this is to collaborate with someone who does something similar to what you do or does something that will complement what you do. For example, if you are selling eco-friendly artwork, you can probably collaborate with a brand that makes eco-friendly paints.

Strategic alliances open up new opportunities to amplify visibility and foster creativity through the sharing of ideas and resources.

Cross promotions:
Cross-promoting is a promotion technique where you promote what your collaborator is doing and vice versa so that your audience becomes more aware of what they are doing. And this works the other way around. So when you have an audience that you are teaching watercolours to, you can collaborate and promote a brand that sells watercolour paint. That way, you are getting them potential buyers. At the same time, when they promote what you are doing through your collaboration, they are letting their buyers know that you are an artist who also teaches art. Both of

you benefit from this. It creates a win-win situation where both of you reach out to a broader audience and benefit from the shared marketing efforts.

The ROI (Return on Investment) of branding: Measuring Grand Success:
Measuring your brand's success gives you a better idea of how your branding is doing. It involves tracking engagement, website traffic, social media inside sales data, and other relevant indicators that point to which direction your brand is headed. It shows you where you are being more successful and what areas you need to focus on for improvement.

It provides valuable insights into the effectiveness of branding strategies and helps you refine them for optimal results.

Monetizing your brand:
There are different ways in which a strong brand can translate into financial gains. When your brand does really well, you can get increased sales, potentially higher prices, lucrative collaborations, and other revenue streams.

Understanding how branding directly impacts revenue empowers artists to make informed decisions that optimise financial growth and sustainability.

When you strategize and plan your brand around the points that were discussed above, you can have guaranteed success. You can apply these principles to unlock the power of your brand. Branding has a very important role to play in how your products reach customers and how they look at them.

Phew. Look at how far you've come! Good job so far! We will now get back into my story and look at one of the most intense phases I went through that shook my beliefs to the core and became a huge influence on who I am today.

Life-Changing Lessons

While I was working on the project for my friend, I received a panicked call from my mother around 6:30 p.m. Her voice sounded scared, and she urgently asked me to come home. Sensing the seriousness, I hurried back as fast as I could.

As I arrived, I saw my mother sitting near the temple, tears streaming down her face. She was in distress, and I feared the worst. I asked her if something had happened to our father or her. She broke into tears and shared that our father had been in an accident and was unconscious. My brother, who had been called by my mother, arrived soon after. We were devastated and overwhelmed by the seriousness of the situation.

Our father lived 300 kilometres away, and we learned he had taken a lift on a bike, which unfortunately had an accident. He was unconscious and in critical condition. We were scared beyond words, trying to contact people and gather more information. It was a surreal and terrifying moment for us.

I remember that night vividly—the anxiety, fear, and desperation. In a moment of sheer anxiety and challenge to my faith, I told my mom that if her God was real, I wanted my dad to pull through. It was a test of my beliefs and a plea for his recovery.

During those dark days and nights, when the entire country was wearing masks and hiding behind closed doors, we rushed to the ICU at 3:00 AM, clinging to hope and praying for Dad's recovery.

I cannot even begin to express how difficult it was. When I saw my dad lying there, his hands and knuckles bleeding, a big scar on his head, not moving at all, I was utterly devastated. It was painful to see my father in such a state, unsure if he was alive or not. He was my foundation and the epitome of home for me. Without him, it felt like there was no home.

That night was chaos. I was furious, scared, and in agony. Dad had a severe head injury, and despite our efforts, there were no doctors available. We spent the night in tears, with no clarity on whether Dad would make it through. The following days were a blur, filled with fear and uncertainty. The doctors provided no reassurance; instead, they prepared us for the worst, saying that most cases like this did not end well.

We moved him from a small hospital to a bigger one, desperately seeking answers and hope. The doctors could not assure us of his survival. Amid a ward full of other patients, I was adamant that my dad had to live, despite the grim warnings and the painful reality unfolding before me. They asked to prepare for the worst.

I decided that I would stay strong and fight for him to live. I challenged my faith. I told my mother that if the God she believed in was real, he should recover well. Somewhere inside of me, the crying was done.

That was a time of constant effort and immense faith. I reached out to everyone in my network, desperately searching for the best neurosurgeon who could save Dad. I was determined and focused, feeling a sense of power within, as if I were Shiva, certain that I could rescue him. Amidst the uncertainty of life and death, I had this unwavering belief that he would survive. And at that time, a doctor came and gave us a ray of hope. That was when I realised that when you truly love something with all your heart, things will work out.

I shared our ordeal on social media, expressing the raw reality of what we were going through. The response was overwhelming. People from different corners of the world, from Singapore to Israel, extended their prayers and support. It was a beautiful display of love and solidarity, a reminder that in times of adversity, the right people step in. The collective prayers of people can bring about miracles.

Despite the uncertainty and the rollercoaster of emotions, Dad's condition gradually stabilised after three to four days. However, we learned he had suffered half-body paralysis, multiple ligament injuries, and a brain haemorrhage. It was heartbreaking to witness the severity of his injuries. The following months were a blur of staying by Dad's side during the COVID crisis, witnessing his gradual progress and setbacks, enduring surgeries, and seeing the challenges he faced with partial paralysis and injuries. It was an emotionally taxing period that stretched over two and a half to three months, filled with uncertainties about his recovery and the form it would take.

During that tough time, seeing my dad get better was like a rollercoaster of feelings. It was like sailing through unknown waters, not knowing what would happen next. His look changed a lot, and that made me feel a mix of hope and sadness.

I remember a moment when I played Shiv Tandav while he was getting better. It felt like this music was bringing hope when he moved his hand a little. It was like a miracle to me—a moment I will always remember.

As he got better, I held his hand and wrote a message, saying I was going to bring him back. I was hoping he would get back to being himself. It was a touching moment that made me feel grateful and amazed.

But as time passed, I realised he was different physically, and he struggled to remember things we used to do together. It was sad to see him not remember those good times we shared. He could not remember my name. It made me wonder if I wanted the same dad back or someone new.

It was hard to see him struggle with his memory and his body. We switched hospitals, hoping for better care. But even then, it was tough watching him try to get better and remember things. It was a time filled with worries and hoping for the best, but not knowing what would happen next.

This part of my life taught me a lot about staying

strong and never giving up hope, especially when family love is involved. It changed me and showed me how strong love and hope can be in tough times.

We brought my dad back to our city, but things took a turn for the worse when he started losing control over his body. It was like he went back to being a child, not knowing what was happening around him. His condition deteriorated rapidly, and despite our hopes for recovery, two months passed with no improvement. It was scary to see him losing more and more of himself every day.

We rushed him to another doctor, and this time they told us that urgent surgery was necessary. It was his second brain haemorrhage surgery, as the first one did not resolve the issue. His condition worsened with diminishing reflexes, and it seemed like he was losing function on one side of his body. They showed us visuals of the surgery, where they removed the bad blood from his head. It was a sight that was hard to forget.

Eventually, he underwent another operation, and finally, things started to change. It was like a turning point. Gradually, he regained consciousness, said my name, and his memory started to return. It appeared that the accumulated blood pressure was the true cause of the issue all along.

After that surgery, the real miracle happened when he emerged from the operating room. I was counting every passing hour, anxiously waiting for him to open his eyes after that second surgery. It was this test of patience from the divine, giving us what we asked for but with these incredibly tough challenges. Things began to improve drastically. It was like the dark days were finally coming to an end, and there was a sense of relief and hope in the air. It is like a story that could happen to anyone, you know? That moment when you are pushed into fight or flight mode hits hard. When the doctor said my dad might not make it, my mind immediately switched to this mode, where I started preparing myself for the worst.

As the eldest in the family, I felt this immense responsibility to take care of everyone. I had to be strong for them, even though, on the inside, I was completely shattered. I would hide my emotions and offer my shoulder to my mom and my brother, trying to keep them together while breaking inside.

It is a whole different struggle when it is someone you have always looked up to and suddenly you see them in such a vulnerable state. You find yourself in this state of denial, almost bargaining with God, challenging the situation.

It is a tough battle when you are faced with such uncertainties, fighting your own battles while negotiating with a higher power.

This was my time of challenging God, a period where I laid down this ultimatum that my dad must return the same way he was or even better. I wouldn't accept anything less. I believe God is compassionate and presents himself when the right moment arrives.

In our case, none of us contracted COVID during those trying months. It was a period filled with prayers from friends and family, which I believe produced incredible miracles right in front of my eyes. It was a time when the worst and the best moments collided, and I cannot fathom anything better or worse than that.

I strongly believe that the good karma you put out in the world returns in various forms for yourself and your loved ones. I pray that I can be a vessel for those who need help, especially for fellow artists or anyone who needs support. I sometimes reflect on the what-ifs—what if we had no money for the operation, what if something happened to my mom due to the shock—yet somehow, everything fell into place at the right time, saving my dad's life. It reinforces my belief in karma and the power of positive actions in the world.

This experience changed me profoundly, nudging me out of my comfort zone. Witnessing a life-and-death situation transformed me and my brother into adults almost overnight. We made decisions for our parents for the first time. It was time for us to become more responsible. My brother matured 10 times, and his business grew 100 times. I have learned that I never want anyone, especially my loved ones, to experience anything as distressing as what we went through. I am just grateful he is back and doing better now.

At that time, I decided to leave art. I was done with art. I had to do something else to make money. My brother's business suffered due to the pandemic; my father was still recovering, and my artwork was not going anywhere. It stagnant. I decided that when my dad recovered and returned to the office, I would leave my house. I felt that I was too attached to him, and attachment leads to disappointment.

He recovered well and returned to work. The day he left, I left for my go-to-second home. Goa. I suddenly felt empowered from within. I felt powerful and ready to face anything that life was going to throw at me. My father had just recovered from a terrible accident; my business was done, and I just left.

Goal Again!

So, when I landed in Goa after my dad returned to work, it was a time of intense self-reflection. That phase of the second year of the COVID-19 era, spanning 2021–2022, marked a transformative phase in my life. It was during this time in Goa that I experienced a sort of spiritual awakening. It was an opportunity for me to understand why I made certain choices and to tap into a newfound energy, feeling ready to take on the world.

I think awakenings are not sweet; they are like slaps from all sides. I had an awakening in Goa. My life took me on a rollercoaster of discoveries. I learned how to live independently while still cherishing my family. It was like finding this sweet spot where love and detachment harmoniously coexisted, bringing me immense happiness.

That time in Goa was a game-changer for me. I discovered this life coach, Puja Punit, from Chennai. Investing in her programme was like investing in myself for the first time. I was in full self-improvement mode meditating, munching on healthy food, and focusing a lot on healing.

Now, if you are wondering how I managed financially in Goa, well, I did not have heaps of cash, but I had some. I thought, Why not try selling my art? I painted a few pieces every month, sometimes just one or two. They sold well! Goa is a gold mine for artists; there is always someone eager to buy cool artwork, especially with all the new places popping up.

The funny thing is, whenever I felt like giving up on art, it somehow found its way back to me, making me fall in love with it all over again. It is like this crazy love-hate relationship where even if I try to ditch art, it is like, "Nope, I'm sticking around." Art has been a constant source of inspiration and motivation for me, and it never fails to surprise me with its support. Art finds me; I find art.

During that time in Goa, I was on a creative roll. I started this series of nude paintings. After what had happened with Dad, I began asking questions like, Why do we hide our bodies? What is the big deal with nudity? I mean, when it boils down to it, what are we taking with us when we leave this world, right?

As I dove into these paintings, something pretty incredible happened. I began to appreciate my own body more. It was like a transformational journey. And you know what? The more I improved in my art, the more empowered I felt. And here is the cool part: when I shared these artworks—and they were nudes, mind you there were mixed reactions. Some people had issues, judgements—you name it.

But in Goa, I found this incredible community that valued authenticity. They were all about accepting yourself just the way you are. Whether you are big, small, cute, or not so cute, it is all about accepting yourself, and that, my friend, leads to a boost in confidence.

Also, being in Goa was such a big part of my healing journey. I met these wonderful people who were so caring, not just for other humans but even for stray animals. It was such an eye-opener. They helped me heal from my dad's trauma and my own past struggles with body image.

You know, all those years of people saying I was fat or chubby—it did a number on me. But gradually, I began to accept myself more. It was a phase of incredible self-awareness and acceptance of my beautiful body. Goa truly changed things for me in more ways than one.

And Puja Punit's course gave me direction. It was something about healing. That healing course turned into coaching mastery. Until then, I had never imagined myself as a coach. I think Puja unknowingly planted a seed in my mind. She was like this flawless goddess who rescued me from all my confusion.

Confusion was my worst enemy back then—how to make money, build a sustainable business, or even create a lifestyle that truly fit. I had to start from scratch.

And then this idea popped up: what if I could educate people? Conduct online workshops, teach them art, or maybe explore other possibilities.

Suddenly, I felt this pull towards serving others. I wanted to find a way to make a difference. That programme did not immediately change things, but it definitely did leave a mark on me. It got me thinking about coaching as a career path because I absolutely love helping people, and at the same time, I love to paint.

After a few months, there was a significant change

inside me. Something clicked, and I began seeing things differently. It was kind of like a lightbulb moment!

The Mystery Man!
(Underworld to Innerworld)

Now this story is real and not at the same time. If you like to imagine fictional stories, you can; if you do not, you do not need to. Think of it as a goofy dream. But I would like to tell you a story. This is the story of how I met (or did I?) this man, who played a very important part in my journey (or did he?).

Let us imagine an old man with a rockstar vibe, riding a cool bike. He had pretty long hair and kept smoking all the time. We will call him Baba 2.

He gave out different vibes. He liked to hang out with beautiful young girls. He was just chilling. He would treat the ladies to good food and all the nice things at his place. But somewhere, there was more to his intentions than he showed. Something we would not realise the first few times we met him.

I was targeted by him too. He had quite the history and had a lot of very interesting stories to tell. He had had some interesting experiences in life. He claimed to have been an evil person but did tear up, saying he was a changed man. His story could be a book in itself.

I felt like there were two sides to this experience: a good side and a bad side. The good side held a caring, wise aspect, wishing for everyone's happiness and well-being, yet the other side was obscure, with unclear intentions. It was strange.

There was a weird vibe that did not feel right around his house. The energies simply did not feel safe after a while. Weird things would happen every time I tried to leave his place. The bike would run out of petrol and I would have to return to his house; the mobile would run out of charge or network; maps would stop working; and I would sprain my leg. Bad things would just start happening, like obstacles to stop me from going, and I would have to return to him.

He had also said that he knew magic. I did not know if that was to be believed or not, like in this story, but as I have mentioned, the energy simply did not feel right. He would also pray to God at the same time. So I was confused. It felt like I was under a spell, like he was doing something to my energies. There was something dark around his aura. But he was a very interesting character among those whom I met.

While there, I found myself resorting to chanting my prayers. I had to cling to the source of light because I did not know who else to ask for help from. So my connection with Siva became stronger after this. I wanted to go back home and somehow find a way out of there. I finally did go home.

During that phase, I went through a Dark Night of the Soul phase, losing friends and family temporarily, a time that acted as a reset. It was a period of self-reflection, confronting both the positive and negative aspects within me. The darkness within allowed me to see my light, embracing complete self-acceptance, and acknowledging the balance between the two. Gradually, I realised that life is not about categorising good and bad but about understanding the equanimity and balance between them. This phase took me six months.

He taught me to check my connection with the universe every time I felt disconnected or scared. I learned to start having a conversation with Siva, build that connection with Him, and believe that He will do everything for me. I think that is what led me to my awakening.

I found myself through this, and it was like a reflection of my own negativity. It was then that I learned that we need to go through these emotions and face our own darkness to fully see and embrace our light and ourselves. Not many of us are comfortable showing ourselves to ourselves. This phase made me face the other side of myself that I had not been ready to accept, which was also me until then. Like putting together the dark and light without any judgment. This comes back to the balance between the good and bad in the world and infinity.

And this lesson is something that has stayed with me ever since.

Embarking on a new
journey

During these six months, nearly at the brink of bankruptcy, I invested my last penny in coaching. Struggling to decide what to teach online, I reflected on my experiences. Having gone through confusion myself, I understood the struggle of starting an online venture and figuring out what to teach. I realised that healing had been the focal point of my journey, from assisting my father's healing to my personal healing in Goa. It became clear that I wanted to help others with their healing processes. Another small investment in a coach led me to this realisation, marking a significant turning point in my path.

Between July and January, I embarked on a journey of self-improvement, investing my time and resources into learning coaching systems and understanding the intricacies of setting up a business. However, by January 22, 2022, on my brother's birthday, the situation was dire. My bank account showed a negative balance of 984 rupees (-$12). It was a moment of stark realisation—the feeling of having no money in the bank was an overwhelming and soul-crushing experience. It was a sensation that surpassed all the lows I had encountered before.

At that moment, I felt utterly alone, unable to rely on my family for financial support. Despite my unwavering trust in my coach and the systems I was learning, the absence of money to invest in myself amplified the sense of despair. I found myself seeking solace in a temple, with tears streaming down my face, pouring out my heart to Shiva, the deity I believed in. It was a moment of raw vulnerability, a plea for a significant and transformative change in my life.

It was a point of complete exhaustion, emotionally drained from the rollercoaster of life's constant ups and downs. I stood there, desperate for a breakthrough, silently begging for a shift in my circumstances, and earnestly praying for divine intervention to alter the trajectory of my life.

Instead of support, I faced a piercing blow to my spirit. He, being younger and seemingly more financially successful, called me a "loser." It cut through me deeply—being branded as such by my younger brother felt like a sharp stab to my pride. The resentment and frustration welled up inside me, igniting a determination to prove him wrong. I made a silent vow to myself that day: "I'm going to show you."

That month, amidst the shattered emotions, I made a conscious decision—I would take up the challenge. No more surrendering to despair. I began my transformation by dedicating myself to learning new skills every morning. At 9:00 AM sharp, I buried myself in the world of copywriting, marketing, crafting irresistible offers using words, mastering Facebook ads, and embracing the mindset of a savvy entrepreneur.

With unwavering commitment, I absorbed the teachings of my mentors, internalising their business principles. It was not just about acquiring knowledge; it was about absorbing a mindset that would enable me to soar higher. The mindset shift became pivotal in my journey. I invested a significant sum, my last one lakh rupees ($1200), to learn from mentors. However, it was not solely about the strategies they imparted.

The investment did not just unlock knowledge; it unlocked an empowering mindset shift that propelled me forward. I realised that it was not about the specific techniques taught; it was about the strategic mindset that helped me envision the potential to generate ten times that investment monthly. It was not just a financial return; it was a mental elevation, a shift that powered my journey towards a ten lakh per month goal. The secret was not solely in what was taught; it lay in the transformative power of the mindset cultivated during that transformative learning phase.

As we climb a little higher, there is something more you need to know about how effective having a growth mindset can be for you to grow as a successful artist and become a smartpreneur. Enough of the small steps. It is now time to take a huge leap. Let me guide you towards having a growth mindset.

Growth Mindset

Embracing a growth mindset is not just a choice. It is a very important decision that sets apart aspiring artists from those who truly flourish in this vast world of art.

"So what exactly is a growth mindset?" you might ask.

A growth mindset, the belief that abilities and intelligence can be developed through dedication and hard work, holds the key to unlocking an artist's fullest potential. It is how you look at and accept the possibility of expansion in terms of creativity and your skillset.

In this chapter, we will look at fictional examples and look into the reasons why artists should wholeheartedly adopt this mindset, supported by compelling stories and a powerful framework that validates its effectiveness.

Continuous learning and improvement:

A growth mindset pushes artists towards a path of continual learning and improvement. Just like how a seed grows into a huge tree with nurturing and time, the artist does too and matures with dedicated effort and perseverance.

Meet Sarah, a self-taught painter, initially facing doubts about her abilities, she shifted her perspective, viewing challenges as opportunities for growth. With every critique and setback, she learned and evolved. Each painting became a testament to her dedication and the power of a mindset centred on growth.

You need to nurture your business and put in the effort required to constantly evolve.

Resilience in the Face of Challenges:

The art world can be a demanding arena, often filled with rejection and criticism. Artists with a growth mindset perceive challenges as stepping stones, not stumbling blocks.

Consider the story of Arjun, a sculptor. Despite facing a series of disappointments with art exhibitions, he viewed each rejection as a valuable lesson. With grit and determination, he refined his sculptures, incorporating feedback and improving with each creation. His resilience bore fruit when his sculptures were not only accepted but celebrated at a prestigious exhibition.

When someone gives their suggestions and criticises your work, take it as constructive criticism and give it some serious thought. If you feel that it is valuable and helps improve your work, apply it to your work and see how it looks. If you think it does not, then just thank them for their suggestion and go on. Do not get disappointed or upset by such comments. Do not let them bog you down; just keep proceeding on your journey.

Innovation and creativity unleashed:

A growth mindset fuels innovation and creativity. Artists who believe in their capacity to grow are more likely to experiment, take risks, and think outside the conventional boundaries of artistry.

Take the case of Diya, a digital artist. Struggling with a creative block, she decided to learn a new technique. and combined it with her style, creating a series of groundbreaking digital artworks that caught the attention of a renowned art magazine.

What happens most of the time is that we, as

artists, tend to get comfortable with a certain technique or style of art. This can lead to saturation. You may feel bored at some point, or your audience may want to see something new from you. To avoid this from happening, you have to be open to learning something new. You have to be open to experimenting. Do not be afraid of your canvas. Be bold and try something you have not done before. Learn a new skill that will help you improve your art.

You will not know unless you try. So do not stop yourself.

Framework: The Cycle of Growth and Achievement

This is how you will do things if you are an artist with a growth mindset.

- **Challenge and Effort:**

When you encounter a new challenge or a new project, it ignites your passion, pushing you to put in more effort and dedication to tackle it.

- **Learning and adaptation:**

You actively seek to learn and adapt, acquiring new skills and knowledge to overcome the challenge.

- **Mastery and Growth:**

Through sustained effort and learning, you achieve mastery and experience personal growth. This in turn boosts your self-confidence and belief in your own abilities.

- **Success and recognition:**

When you put these together, this growth cycle often leads to your success, recognition, and further challenges, continuing the cycle of growth and achievement.

Therefore, the power of a growth mindset cannot be underestimated in an artist's journey. It paves the way for a continuous cycle of growth, strength in times of adversity, and groundbreaking creativity. As you embrace this mindset and immerse yourself in this wonderful journey of improvement, you unlock your true potential and leave a permanent mark on the canvas of the art world.

So are you ready to approach your art and art business with a growth mindset?

A shift and a launch

As I embarked on my journey towards transformation and growth, I made an important decision: to venture into coaching. Drawing from my own experiences, I chose to combine two pillars of my life—art and healing. Art had been my constant companion through life's trials; it was there to console me during heartbreaks, to support me when there were financial challenges, and to offer solace when I needed it the most.

It had always been more than a passion; it was an intrinsic part of me, something I indulged in mindlessly, losing track of time in its creative embrace. That was when I realised—my niche was not just an art form or a particular medium; it was the blissful state of being when I immersed myself in artistic expression and connected with that flow that transcended everything else around me. That deep immersion into creativity, where time seemed to stand still, defined my niche—a space where I found solace and absolute fulfilment.

With this realisation, I formulated my coaching niche, a combination of art and healing. Having seen ups and downs in life, I discovered an inner strength that made me determined in my decision to help others heal.

Thus, I designed and launched my first webinar—a transformative journey through mandala for healing. Little did I anticipate the overwhelming response it would receive.

The journey of the first three days of my healing workshop was proof of the power of determination and support. With the guidance and encouragement from my mentors, I successfully launched the workshop, and to my amazement, within this short span, I closed my first deal. However, amidst this professional success, a pivotal moment occurred—one that would forever alter not just my professional path but also my sense of purpose and responsibility towards others.

Puja became my first student to buy my high ticket, which was at that time priced at fifty thousand rupees ($600). She, a single mom, was widowed and was still in pain over losing the love of her life. Seeing the pain that she was in reminded me of what I had experienced not too long ago during the whole incident with my father. Witnessing her anguish resonated deeply within me, and in that reflection, I saw an opportunity to offer solace.

Helping Puja on her journey was a transformative experience for both of us. It was my first high-ticket online coaching programme, and I had minimal experience as a coach, yet she trusted me. Witnessing her progress and growth towards the light was an incredibly empowering moment. It was then that I felt a newfound sense of power within me, realising that I could genuinely help people navigate their own journeys.

She chose to overcome her challenges. Seeing her transformation was profound. I observed her transition from a place of deep despair to rediscovering her smile, her emotional balance, and reclaiming her place in the business world. Her determination to stand tall for herself and her son was nothing short of inspiring.

As she completed the programme, I saw the remarkable changes in her, and her happiness was palpable. She expressed her gratitude, blessing me for the transformative experience. She wished that the next time she would have to meet me, there would be a tonne of people in the queue waiting to meet me before her.

This experience not only impacted her life but immensely influenced mine as well. It solidified my determination to continue coaching and to assist many more individuals on their journeys towards healing, empowerment, and success. The impact of witnessing someone's transformation from darkness to light was a powerful reminder of the purpose and fulfilment coaching could bring to my life.

Today, I reflect on the impact of one client's manifestation and how it transformed my business. Puja's desire for my success was a catalyst. I was not focused on acquiring numerous clients; my attention was solely focused on providing her with the best support. Her desire and her blessings were powerful. Her blessings acted as a catalyst, steering us towards our flourishing state today.

This experience taught me the immense strength of women in business and the importance of women supporting each other. Puja's influence was instrumental in our growth and success. Somewhere, I feel her blessings acted as a catalyst, steering us towards our flourishing state today.

Realising that I wanted to expand my coaching and online business skills, I continued to help people through healing and the art of mandala. My dedication to assisting others in their healing journeys motivated me to take each step forward in learning new skills.

I felt a resonance with business, healing, and art. These were the pillars I wanted my school to revolve around. I strongly believe that these three areas were fundamental for establishing a solid foundation. Healing or nurturing the mindset is crucial for the growth of any venture. Equally important is acquiring business skills and fostering creativity.

The Vision

I was driven by this inclination towards starting this business. However, I found myself in Bangalore for an unexpected reason: to meet a potential partner. Surprisingly, amid establishing my online and offline businesses, there was a desire within me—a longing for love. Aren't we all seeking that connection? This inherent longing guided me to Bangalore in pursuit of love.

I met a guy, a friend for a year or two, with whom I had engaged in countless virtual conversations. The time came to meet in person, and that was when I realised the difference between us.

He was a software engineer who spent very little time doing anything else besides his job. Our preferences vastly differed—he was content indoors, immersed in games and computers, while I cherished outdoor activities. It was evident that our paths did not align.

However, this experience served as an eye-opener. Witnessing his unwavering dedication to his job, his financial stability, and his peaceful lifestyle left an impression on me. At a young age, he had invested in real estate, securing a peaceful existence that exuded freedom from financial worries. This encounter ignited a realisation within me during the return flight from Bangalore to Gujarat.

While flying, stripped away from distractions like phones and Wi-Fi, I found clarity in thought. I love flights. I always get the best ideas on my flights because I get the time to contemplate and be creative. I would journal and jot down my thoughts and ideas on my flights.

During those two hours, ideas and reflections poured out onto my journal's pages. It was in those moments that I decided I did not need a man for financial security. I made a firm commitment to provide that security for myself, an epiphany that transformed my perspective.

That flight was a pivotal moment for me, for transformation and renewed vision. Reflecting on my journey so far, I realised the wealth of experience I had amassed in the art field. It struck me that most artists often take years to achieve what I had accomplished at a relatively young age. During that flight, a memory surfaced: Vision Uncle. His teachings resurfaced in my mind, inspiring a new vision for myself.

I decided my vision would now focus on assisting artists to surpass my achievements or evolve even further in their careers. My aim shifted to supporting artists in their business endeavours, moving past any remaining sense of competition or envy. Determined, I returned home with a newfound vision for myself.

Within a week, I launched my business. Drawing from my previous experiences, I knew how to orchestrate a successful launch. I had a network, leads, and the skill to bring ideas to life. As I navigated this new direction, I realised that I had become an expert in launching offers, capable of helping anyone launch their business, be it online or offline, crafting an offer within minutes.

The idea took shape, and I launched a three-day art business challenge—an opportunity for others to experience this transformation firsthand. If you would like to experience the same, come join my three-day Art Business Challenge. The link is at the end of the book.

In fact, for all you readers, as I write this on Black Friday, let me give you a free link to my art marketing webinar. Do watch it.

So, picture this: it was June 2022, around the time of my birthday. That was when I took the plunge and hosted my very first webinar. Honestly, I was feeling a bit shaky about it all. I mean, who wouldn't be, right? I started off with a price tag of eighteen thousand rupees ($216) for the program. After launching the Silver programme, a three-month initiative, things took an exciting turn. It was quite underpriced. But I did close a few deals, and I made a total of ninety-five thousand rupees ($1140).

I guess that beginner's hesitation paid off big time. It was a crazy ride, but sometimes taking that leap of faith, even when you are unsure, can lead to the most mind-blowing results.

After closing that remarkable ninety-five thousand rupee deal, I decided to make a big change: I packed my bags and headed straight for Bangalore. It was not just about the money; it was about seeking a fresh start and independence.

Family dynamics played a role too; there was not much support for my art and business endeavours. So, I made the decision to break away and focus on creating my own path.

With extensive research and hard work, I finally unlocked the secret formula for launching an online business. This move was important, marking a significant shift in both my digital pursuits and my artistic business. It opened up a whole new world of opportunities, each carrying its own silver lining.

My move to Bangalore marked a shift in focus, from personal adjustments to catering to the first ten individuals who placed their trust in my online art business program. For the initial three months, I dedicated myself solely to serving these ten remarkable individuals, guiding them through monetizing their art.

What struck me most was realising that these artists encountered similar challenges that I once faced.

They struggled with launching themselves online, starting classes, selling their art, pricing their creations, managing commissioned pieces, drafting proposals, and handling payments.

It was as if I was reliving my initial struggles through them; their questions mirrored the ones I had encountered since day one of assisting artists. Addressing over 10,000 repeating questions over time enabled me to understand the pain points thoroughly. I devoted time to each individual, resolving their queries and providing tailored guidance.

I have always held onto the belief of nurturing a sense of family within my community and providing unwavering support to my mentees to help them flourish.

One of the most frequently asked questions from many artists, even to this day, is about pricing. All of us go through that phase of being confused as to how we must charge for our artwork. Worry not, for I am here. Let me take your hand as we take another step and learn that you can price your art.

Pricing

Pricing your art

Pricing your artwork can be very confusing and tricky to decide. Unlike other products, where you can compare prices, art does not work that way. Because every art has a different value that depends on various factors that simply cannot be compared.

There will come a time in your art journey when you will have to slowly start increasing your prices. It is a strategic process that involves considering a lot of factors, some of which include:
- The value of your work,
- The market demand,
- Your reputation and
- The cost associated with creating and selling your art.

So we will look at the steps that will help you navigate this process and effectively raise your price as an artist.

Evaluate your work's value and quality:
When you look at your art and evaluate the value of your work, you will have to be able to assess
- The quality,
- The uniqueness and
- Demand that you have for your artwork.
- Factor in the skill level,
- Materials used,
- The time that you invested in creating it and
- The overall appeal of your creations.

Research the markets:
Another important thing that you will have to do when you are valuing your artwork is to do thorough research in the market and understand what other artists with a similar style as yours, experience, and reputation are charging for their work.

One good place to look for it is Etsy, where you can find a lot of artists who put up their work for sale. You can find artists who have a similar style to yours and check their pricing. You can figure out what works for your products as well. This will give you a benchmark for setting your prices.

Consider your expenses:

Just because you are doing art does not mean you do not spend anything on creating it. So you will have to calculate all the costs involved in creating your art, and these costs include the cost of your materials and the rent you pay for your studio, the utilities, the amount you spend on marketing, and your desired income. Ensure that your prices cover both your costs and provide a reasonable profit margin for you.

Factor in your time and effort:

Art takes time, and time is money. Determine an hourly rate that you feel is right for you. Based on the time and effort you put into creating each of your pieces, multiply this rate by the number of hours that you spend on each piece to account for your time.

For example, with the global market in mind, if you are charging $20 an hour and an art piece takes you 10 hours to make, then you simply multiply 20 by 10, which gives you $200. This is what you will charge for your time. This is just one part of the total amount that you will be charging for your art.

Gradually increase your price. You may start off with $10 an hour or $20 an hour, but you cannot always keep selling your art at that same price. You will have to gradually increase it. A sudden increase may be difficult for your customer base to understand because, when you start selling your artwork at a certain price range, you attract customers who are willing to spend the same on your artwork. However, when you suddenly increase your prices, your current customer base, which is used to the previous price range, will not be ready for the sudden change.

Therefore, it has to be gradual, and one way to do it is by increasing 10% to 20% annually every few years which will allow for a smooth transition.

Communicate value:
Most artists, if not all, would definitely have had to face situations in which they would have had to explain or justify the cost of their work. This is because sometimes people do not understand the value of your art. Therefore, you need to clearly communicate the value, story, and inspiration behind each of your artworks to justify your pricing. You do not have to apologise for your pricing, but they will have to know that they are not just paying for an artwork; they are paying for the overall experience that you are selling along with your artwork. Emphasise the emotional and artistic value that customers receive from owning your art piece.

Build a strong portfolio:
Your portfolio is more or less like a record book of your artwork through the years. So when you

constantly improve your skills and create a portfolio that showcases the growth and mastery of your artistic style, people will understand that this is how much time and effort you have put into it. They will be able to see how much you have grown since you started. That way, they will understand the value of your art. A strong, well-planned portfolio can justify higher prices.

Establish your brand and reputation:
You have to be able to invest in building your brand and reputation through exhibitions, collaborations, awards, or featured articles. When you become a reputable artist, you can command higher prices due to the perceived value of your artwork. There is a reason certain people pay a lot higher prices for certain brands compared to similar products from a less-reputed brand.

Offer limited editions and exclusive pieces:
When you create a sense of exclusivity and scarcity by creating and offering limitations and one-of-a-kind pieces at higher price points, art collectors will want to buy them because they value uniqueness and rarity. They like investing in products that are not commonly available everywhere, so create limited additions and offer them at higher prices. You can say it is only available for a limited period of time, or there are only so many pieces available of it.

Provide clear pricing structures:
You will have to display your prices clearly and professionally in art galleries, online platforms, and art exhibitions to avoid any unnecessary confusion that may arise. Transparency helps build trust with potential buyers. So make sure you have your pricing planned well and clearly displayed for your buyers to see.

Educate your audience:
Before you give them the chance to question your prices or the value of your art, it would be advisable to educate your audience about the process that is involved in creating your art piece. It can be your artistic process, the materials you use, and the dedication it takes to create each piece because many people see the results and may think it is just an abstract painting, so it does not take that much time to create. As an artist, you know what goes into creating a certain art piece. So when you educate them on this, it can help them understand the value behind the prices.

Get Feedback:
Do not hesitate to seek feedback from trusted colleagues and existing clients before implementing price changes. Asking them for feedback can help you understand whether your prices are justified. You can figure out if you can work out something that would work for both you and the end buyers and not come across as overly

expensive or overly cheap. Their insights can be valuable in making informed decisions.

If you plan your pricing with these points in mind, you will be able to price your art correctly. In FAT World School, we look at this in detail.

Getting back to my story, I started seeing the success stories of my mentees. Swetha, a housewife turned artist, is now taking bulk corporate orders and doing exhibitions all across the country.

Smriti, a former lawyer turned housewife turned artist, is judging art shows, showcasing her art at exhibitions in her city, and inspiring young talents in her city.

These stories are just a glimpse; from the beginning, I sensed the programme's profound impact, transforming the very essence of individuals aspiring to embrace their
artistic talents. Witnessing these transformations, I realised the true power of this programme in reshaping the dynamics of the art industry.

As I walked alongside these ten incredible individuals, I learned invaluable lessons about fostering a strong community. These experiences taught me the true potential a community holds. It is not just about support; it is about the transformative strength of a community offers. As I walked alongside these ten incredible individuals, I learned invaluable lessons about fostering a strong community. These experiences taught me the true potential a community holds. It is not just about support; it is about the transformative strength a community offers.

Allow me to take your hand and showcase how being part of a community can be an extraordinary game-changer.

Community

Community Building

Community building as an artist is crucial for several reasons. A strong and engaged community can provide support, inspiration and opportunities for growth in your artistic career. Fellow artists can help give you suggestions, answer your art queries and help you find material when you do not know where to look for. Additionally, it helps you establish a brand, increase your reach and ultimately monetise your artistic endeavours. Here is why community building is important and how you can go about it.

Importance of Community Building:
Support and Encouragement:
A community of fellow artists and art enthusiasts can provide encouragement, constructive feedback and emotional support during

challenging times. This kind of support is crucial for maintaining motivation and resilience in your artistic journey.

Networking opportunities:

Building a community allows you to connect with other artists, potential clients, art collectors, gallery owners, and influencers. These connections can lead to collaborations, exhibitions, commissions, and other monetization opportunities.

Increase the visibility:

Engaging with a community helps increase your visibility within the art world, and exposure to a wider audience can result in more opportunities for sales and recognition.

Diversified Skill Sets:

Interacting with a diverse community exposes you to different artistic styles, techniques, and perspectives. This exposure can help you expand your skill set and creativity.

Validation and feedback:

Community provides a platform for receiving validation and feedback on your work. Helping you understand what resonates with your audience and potential buyers and where you can improve.

Marketing and Promotion:

An engaged community can become your brand

ambassador, spreading the word about your art, exhibitions, and events, effectively marketing, and promoting your work.

How do you build a community and monetise it?
Engage on social media:
Use platforms like Instagram, YouTube, Facebook, Twitter, and LinkedIn to showcase your artwork. Share the art process, engage with your audience, and connect with other artists and art enthusiasts.

Start a blog or a vlog:
Create a blog or a vlog related to your artistic journey, offering insights, tutorials, and behind-the-scenes looks into your process. When people are able to connect with the kind of person you are, you can attract followers and position yourself as an authority in your niche.

Participate in art communities:
Join online forums, art groups, or social media groups related to your artistic style and medium. Engage in discussions. Share your work and provide value to others by being there for them.

Collaborate with other artists:
Collaborate with fellow artists on joint projects, art exhibitions, or social media campaigns. It not only expands your reach but also introduces your work to a new audience.

Host workshops and webinars:
Offer workshops, webinars, or online classes where you teach your artistic techniques and charge a fee for participation to monetize your knowledge and expertise.

Leverage email marketing:
Build an email list by offering a freebie (an art guide, an e-book, or exclusive content) and then regularly engage with your subscribers. Use email newsletters to update them on your art, upcoming events, and promotions.

Create a Patreon or Membership Programme:
Offer exclusive content, early access to new artwork, and personalised experiences to patrons or members who support your work through platforms like Twitter or on your own website.

Sell artwork online:
Set up an online store on your website or use online art marketplaces to sell your artwork to a global audience. Use your community to drive traffic to your online store.

Attend art events and exhibitions:
Attend art fairs, exhibitions, and industry events to connect with fellow artists, gallery owners, collectors, and potential buyers. Networking in person can be highly valuable.

Provide Commissions:
Offer commission-based work, where you create custom pieces based on clients' preferences. Commissioned art can be a significant source of income.

Monetizing your community:
Monetizing your community as an artist involves leveraging the relationships and following you have built to generate income. Here are effective strategies to monetize your community.

Sell your artwork:
Directly sell your artwork and prints of your artwork and merchandise to your community through your website, online marketplaces, or at art exhibitions, and offer exclusive or limited edition pieces to create a sense of scarcity and urgency.

Provide Commissions:
Offer commission services to your community, allowing them to request custom artwork tailored to their preferences. Charge a fee for your time, effort, and expertise in creating personalised pieces.

Create online courses:
Develop and sell comprehensive online courses and tutorials covering various aspects of art, such as painting techniques, digital art, or creative

workshops. Websites like Skillshare, Domestika, Udemy, and YouTube are good for you to make money through your online courses.

Affiliate Marketing:

Partner with art supply companies, art book publishers, or relevant products in your niche to promote products in your community. Earn a commission for every sale made through your unique affiliate link.

Collaborate with brands:

Collaborate with brands related to the art industry or your niche, create sponsored content or cobranded products, and monetize these partnerships.

Licencing and Merchandising:

Licence your art to be used on various products, such as apparel. Home decor, stationery, or accessories. You can also create branded merchandise featuring your artwork for sale.

Art Auctions for Fundraisers:

Host online or offline art auctions, with a portion of the proceeds donated to a charitable cause. Engage your community to bid on and purchase the artwork.

Add Subscription Boxes:

Curate and offer subscription boxes that include a

selection of your artwork, prints, or merchandise. Subscribers pay a regular fee to receive these curated items.

Art Counselling Services:
Offer consulting services to help clients. Choose artwork for their homes and businesses. Charge a fee for personalised art recommendations and guidance.

Crowd-sourced Art Projects:
Involve your community in collaborative art projects, where they contribute ideas, designs, or elements to create a collective artwork. Sell the resulting piece or prints.

Event Hosting on Sponsorship:
Organise art events, exhibitions, or workshops and monetize them through ticket sales, even sponsorships and event fees.

Remember to communicate the value and exclusivity of the monetized offerings to your community and ensure that your strategies align with your brand and the interests of your audience. Additionally, maintain transparency and engagement to build trust and encourage ongoing support from your community.

Fast and Effective Ways to Build Community:
Building a community quickly involves leveraging

effective strategies to attract and engage individuals who share a common interest, passion, or goal. Here are some fast ways to build a community:

Leverage social media:
Utilise platforms like Instagram, Facebook, Twitter, and LinkedIn to create profiles or pages dedicated to your community. Share engaging content, interact with your audience, and encourage them to invite others with similar interests.

Host webinars or live streams:
Organise webinars, live streams, or Q&A sessions on topics relevant to your community's interests. Promote these events through social media, email newsletters, and relevant online forums to attract participants.

Run Contests and Giveaways:
Host contests or giveaways with enticing prizes related to your community's interests. Encourage participants to invite others, follow your page, or share content to increase visibility and attract more members.

Collaborate with influencers:
Partner with influencers or individuals with a significant following in your niche. They can help promote your community to their audience, driving new members to join.

Optimise SEO for your community website:
Ensure your community website is search engine optimised with relevant keywords, meta descriptions, and quality content. This will help potential members find your community through search engine results.

Leverage email marketing:
Use your existing email list or collaborate with similar niche email lists to promote your community. Offer incentives for joining, such as exclusive content or discounts, to encourage sign-ups.

Create valuable content:
Regularly publish valuable, informative, and engaging content related to your community's interests. Share it across social media, forums, and relevant websites to attract individuals looking for that kind of content.

Utilise online forums and communities:
Engage in discussions and share your expertise in online forums, social media groups, or community websites related to your niche. Provide helpful insights and subtly promote your community.

Offer exclusive access:
Provide early access, special features, or exclusive content to the first members who join your community.

Highlight these benefits to encourage early sign-ups.

Leverage paid advertising:
Use paid advertising through platforms like Facebook Ads, Google Ads, or Instagram Ads to target a specific audience interested in your community's topic. Create compelling ad copies and visuals to capture their attention.

Promote Offline:
Use traditional methods like flyers, business cards, or advertisements in local newspapers or magazines to promote your community, especially if it has a local or geographic focus.

Attend relevant events:
Attend conferences, exhibitions, or networking events related to your niche. Engage with attendees, distribute business cards, and share information about your community.

Offer Referral Incentives:
Encourage your current community members to refer new members by offering them incentives, discounts, or other perks for successful referrals.

Engage with Similar Communities:
Engage with and contribute to other communities or social media groups related to your niche. Offer valuable insights and subtly promote your

community as a valuable resource.

Remember to maintain consistent and genuine engagement with your community members to keep them actively involved and attract new members. Providing valuable content, fostering discussions, and responding to their needs and interests will help sustain and grow your community over time.

As for my story, from starting with figures in the five-digit range, our community expanded, and within a short span, we saw our numbers surge into six figures. With growing confidence in our ability to assist artists, our second batch attracted more students, nearly tripling to 30 participants.

The community's growth was unstoppable, leading to our current count of over 100 students, now thriving as Gold members. It was at this point that we introduced our latest programme, MBA Gold, short for Millionaire Business Artist Gold, a cutting-edge initiative tailored for artists who aim for business success.

This programme, launched in 2023, is designed as a six-month course but can extend into a comprehensive one-year diploma. For those interested in joining this transformative programme, a one-on-one call with a member of my team can be easily booked through the link provided at the end.

The QR code for it is on the next page.

Let me guide you through why opportunities for artists are not just increasing but are bound to grow endlessly. This is why becoming an artist now is crucial. The upcoming 'Golden Age' is for us.

Scan Code

The Golden Age

The Golden Age for Artists: Seizing the Opportunity

Welcome to a very crucial point in your journey as an artist. Here, we will delve into the thriving era for artists—a true golden age, if we might call it—of creativity and possibility. As an art business coach, I am here to reveal to you the ample number of opportunities available in this period that we are living in. I will provide you with concrete facts and figures that will help embolden your path on this beautiful journey that you have decided to take as an artist. Congratulations on taking this first step. It is not easy to decide to go this way, and you have done it.

The Digital Revolution: A Global Canvas at Your Fingertips:

In this era, the digital realm has indeed become

an expansive canvas for artists. Before the onset of this digital revolution, the reach all artists had was very minimal. For someone from the other end of the world to be able to even see one's art was almost never heard of (unless the artist was very well known internationally), let alone buy their art. It was absolutely not an easy feat. However, welcome to 2023: a time where everything is easily available, just a touch of a key away. The reach the artists have today with their audience is something that one could have only probably dreamed of back then.

Let us take one platform, Instagram, for example. Think about this: as of this year, 2023, Instagram, one of the leading platforms for artists, boasts over 2.3 billion monthly active users. This gives the artists an unparalleled opportunity to showcase their work and engage with a massive, diverse audience. Can you imagine the number of people who could possibly look at your art through just this platform?! It is amazing, is it not? The power of the internet has reshaped the art world, allowing artists to transcend geographical limits and gain global recognition like never before. This was not even possible a decade ago.

E-Commerce and Art Marketplaces: Direct Access to Your Market.
Now, because of this revolution, e-commerce has naturally experienced an astounding surge, and

the art market is no exception. In 2022, the global online art market will account for approximately $14.38 billion. Platforms like Etsy, tailored for artists and artisans, witnessed a substantial increase in sales. This gives buyers a larger range of art products to choose from.

For example, one can easily purchase authentic, physical art pieces or download digital files sitting at their home or on the go from anywhere in the world. It will be delivered to them in a matter of days or instantly, depending on what they choose and how they make their purchase. Moreover, art marketplaces like Saatchi Art reported a surge in online sales, reinforcing the notion that artists now have direct access to a broader market and a chance to retain a higher percentage of their earnings.

Diverse Revenue Streams: Monetizing Your Multifaceted Talent

The modern age offers artists a plethora of revenue streams beyond traditional art sales. According to a survey by the Freelancers Union and Upwork, nearly 59 million Americans freelanced in 2020, contributing $1.2 trillion to the economy. That has given a brilliant opportunity for artists who are leveraging this gig economy, offering services such as:

- Commissioned artworks,
- Selling NFTs,
- Art workshops,
- and teaching art online.

Additionally, licencing and merchandising agreements present lucrative opportunities for artists to monetize their art beyond the canvas. You now do not have to worry about only having to make money by selling originals. The time taken and the number of pieces you can make and sell is very limited if you depend solely on that as your source of income. With the options mentioned above, you have an array of ways to bring in some passive and active income through art.

Technology and Tools: Empowering Artistic Innovation:

Technological advancements have had a remarkable impact on the art world. Digital tools and software, coupled with the rise of online art academies and tutorials, have democratised the learning of art. Online art sales increased by 16% last year, demonstrating the growing demand for digital art. Artists are now using technology to experiment with animation, digital art, animation, VR, and more. This helps them widen their horizons and interact with an audience that has become more tech-savvy.

Non-fungible tokens, or NFTs, have been one of

the more popular sources of money-making through digital art in the past few years, and we are currently witnessing AI art taking over in popularity. Digitally, your canvas is infinite, and so are the mediums you get to explore. You can also create simple animations with software like Adobe Fresco and Procreate, which are easily available to everyone. YouTube tutorials and videos are other ways you can learn and earn.

The use of technology has also made it possible for more people to learn art and explore the artist in them through online art classes. We now have teachers. say, from India, teaching authentic Madhubani art to students in, say, Australia. The very way these things have become so easily possible is mind-blowing, to say the least.

Community and Collaboration: Strength in Artistic Unity:
Not to generalise, but most artists do not have the opportunity to socialise much because of the very nature of their job. This can lead to feeling disconnected from the outside world and bring about a sense of loneliness. And we people are social animals, and at some point, all of us do need company. In this digital age, artists are no longer isolated in their studios. Online communities and collaboration platforms have seen a surge in participation.

For instance, art-related Facebook groups have witnessed a 48% increase in interactions. This sense of community fosters collaboration, knowledge sharing, and mentorship. A sense of just knowing that you are not alone in this can be very reassuring. Artists can now join forces, not only amplifying their own opportunities but also contributing to the growth and development of the artistic community at large.

Embrace the Golden Age; Seize Your Artistic Destiny:

In this golden age for artists, backed by facts and figures, the possibilities are indeed boundless. The confluence of technology, connectivity, and a global audience has created an exceptional era for creative minds. As your coach and guide, I understand that accepting digitalization can feel intimidating, especially for traditional artists. I encourage you to seize this moment and harness the power of the digital landscape, and cultivate a thriving artistic career. It is possible to find a beautiful balance between the two and to use both to support and push the other to help you grow your career as an artist. This golden age is yours for the taking, so let your creativity shine and your artistry flourish.

Think of MBA Gold not just as a programme but as an investment in securing your golden future.

We can now see the summit. It is breathtaking already, isn't it? This is beautiful! Now, as we climb this final stretch, I will tell you about the various ways you can earn an income from your artwork, using both online and offline sources.

Online and Offline Sources of Income

Online Sources of Income:

NFT Sales:

Creating and selling digital art as NFTs on blockchain platforms like OpenSea, Rarible, or Foundation, where each NFT represents a unique and original piece of digital art.

AI-Generated Artwork Sales:

Developing AI-generated art using algorithms and machine learning techniques and selling it online as digital art or as NFTs.

Digital Art Marketplaces:

Selling your digital artwork or prints of digital art on online platforms dedicated to digital art, such as SuperRare, KnownOrigin, or Mintable.

Online Art Stores:
Operating an online art store on your website, platforms like Etsy, or e-commerce platforms, where you sell original artwork, prints, merchandise, or digital downloads.

Art Commissions (Online):
Accepting commissions for digital art, illustrations, animations, or other creative digital work through online platforms or your own website.

Online Art Courses and Tutorials:
Creating and selling online art courses, tutorials, or workshops covering various art techniques, styles, or software skills.

YouTube and Streaming:
Monetizing your art-related YouTube channel or live streaming your art creation process on platforms like Twitch, where you can earn through ad revenue, sponsorships, and viewer donations.

Art Blogs and Content Creation:
Generating income through blogging about art, sharing insights, art reviews, and tips on your website or other art-related websites.

Offline Sources of Income:
Physical Art Sales:
Selling your original artwork, sculptures, or traditional art pieces in galleries, art shows,

exhibitions, or directly to collectors.

Art Commissions (Offline):
Accepting commissions for traditional art, portraits, murals, or specific art pieces from clients for a fee.

Art Workshops and Classes (Offline):
Conducting in-person workshops, art classes, or demonstrations at local art centres, schools, or community centres, charging a participation fee.

Gallery Representation (Offline):
Partnering with brick-and-mortar art galleries that represent and sell your artwork offline, with the gallery taking a commission from the sales.

Art Fairs and Craft Shows:
Participating in local art fairs, craft shows, or farmers' markets to showcase and sell your artwork to a live, local audience.

By incorporating NFT sales, AI-generated art, and a mix of online and offline income sources, you can diversify your income streams and reach a broader audience, enhancing their overall income and opportunities in the art industry.

Mentee Testimonials

Amber

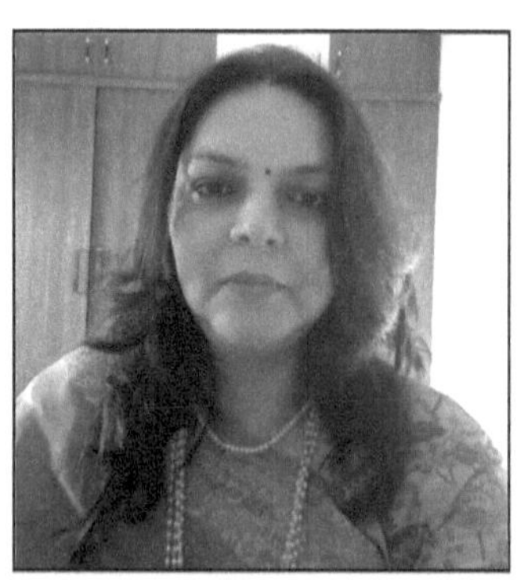

"Hi, I am Amber, Rashmi's student of Artbiz. They say it is only when a student is ready, the real master appears in life... When Rashmi's 'Artbizguru' came into my life there was a paradigm shift in my mind about the art business.

I always knew that the art business would grow with or without me, but a question that I often asked myself was. 'Do I want to grow with the right people and the right mindset?'

I am so grateful to God that I have decided to be with Rashmi. She equipped us with ways to grow in art without sulking and happily enjoying our career on our own ground. Today I am earning good on my own with my art businesses and I am so thankful to Rashmi for holding my hand sometimes, pushing me sometimes and letting us be aware sometimes that it is all worth it. Because I get to be with the right people in the right platform.

Affirming to be in your 100 Rashmi. Thank you so much for being there for whole art community.

Jahanvi. M. Rao

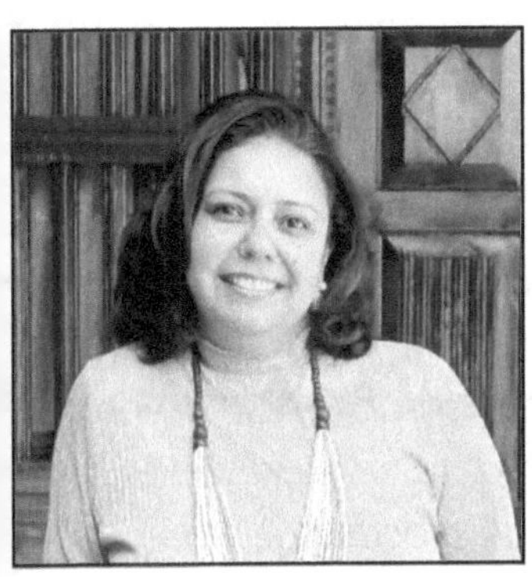

"I am Janhavi M Rao, a crafter based in Mangalore. I have been working very hard to grow my small business and financially establish it for the past 7 years. That was when I came across Rashmi's FAT World School (FWS). Since I joined the school, the feeling

of community and collaboration has given me strength and support.

Rashmi has a whole box (in fact multiple boxes) overflowing with knowledge. Every step we take as artists as we follow what she has already laid out for us, takes us one step closer to our goals. P

I can see myself progressing further every single day. Being with Rashmi is not just a business change it's a lifestyle change and a mindset change, which is like a fuel for growth and progress.

Truly thankful to God for leading me to the FWS. Truly Thankful to Rashmi for starting this venture to help artists find the place they deserve in society."

Anika Khurana

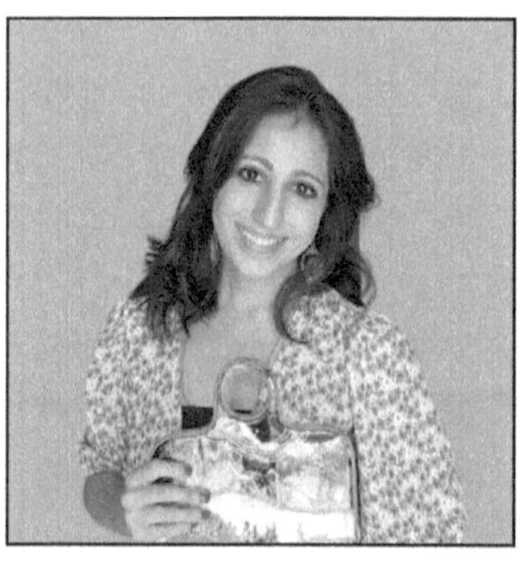

Hi my name is Anika Khurana and I am a resin artist, putting a unique spin on glassware and gift sets. I joined Rashmi as I really wanted to understand how to establish myself as an artist in India. I wanted to venture into large wall art pieces but, was not feeling like I had all the tools to tackle the Indian market. Learning from Rashmi gave me the confidence to step further into the world of art and join the Indian Art Festival. I have learnt many pearls of wisdom and tactics that I feel will continue to grow my business and confidence in the art world. Thank you, Rashmi.

Rima Rahul Asani

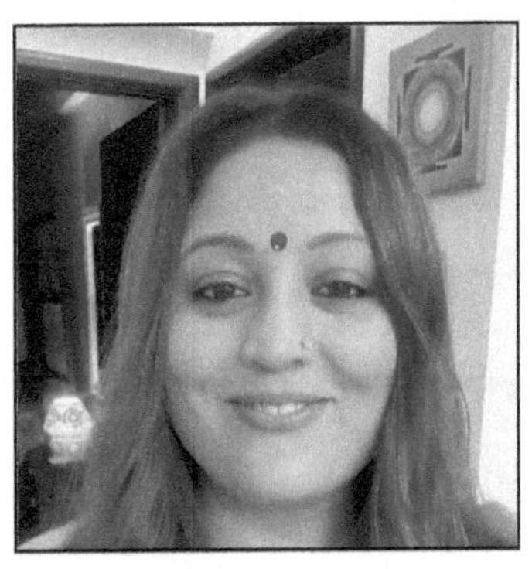

"Rashmi Suthar's transformative guidance redefined my artistic journey. A design school alumnus, I embraced Fine Arts in my 40's after leaving a thriving realty career. Rashmi, a phenomenal mentor, revolutionized my approach. In just six months, her ingenious coaching led me to launch a podcast, cultivate a dreamy Instagram presence, and witness a tenfold surge in sales, predominantly with an international clientele. Her marketing brilliance, coupled with my sales background, propelled my artpreneurial success. Swiftly adapting to AI, I'm grateful for Rashmi's unwavering support. I wish her continued success in all future endeavours."

With love and designer blessings,
Rima Rahul Asani.

Throughout our journey, we have coached over 8,000 artists. I have been exposed to an incredible volume of art, making it an overwhelming task to choose whom to assist. If you are a committed artist and you have followed along until this point, I am here for you. I genuinely invite you to consider joining one of our programs. Whether you are eager to commence or enhance your artistic journey, I am here to support your growth.

I understand the challenges of striving for admission to the best schools globally, especially when finances become a barrier. Whether or not you choose to enrol in all our programmes, I encourage you to explore the opportunities available. For beginners, the Art Business Challenge and the Art Business Silver Membership serve as excellent starting points. However, if you're a dedicated artist seeking transformation, I invite you to book a one-on-one call for our six-month program. This programme has empowered students like Smriti, Ram, and numerous others, propelling them towards success as artists. Here is the QR code for further details.

Scan Code

As we stand on top of this mountain together, can you feel the overwhelming emotion? Embrace this abundance surrounding us— the expansive, clear skies, the soaring birds, the fresh breeze, the earthy scents, and the subtle chill in the air. Everything you once dreamt of is now within your reach. With open arms, you embrace the universe, feeling its warm embrace in return. You acknowledge this beautiful life and realize it is time for us to embrace each other, expressing gratitude for this incredible journey we have shared together.

If you have reached this far and are genuinely serious about taking your art journey further, I would love to meet you in person online. That will be another journey in itself.

Thank you for reading and joining me thus far.
Love,
Rashmi

My Advice

- Don't be cheap on the journey to becoming the best.
- Be a lifelong learner.
- Learn money from a young age; if you haven't done so yet, start now.
- Detach yourself from the outcome in order to manifest your dreams.
- Get business training to fast-forward your growth.
- Invest money in marketing, free is very slow.
- Develop strong networking skills.

Tell me what you think or say hi @artbizguru_official

Book Reccomendations

Be Here Now by Ram Dass

Gita Darshan by Osho

Ashtavakra Gita by Rohan Richards

Steal Like an Artist by Austin Kleon

Profit First: Transform Your Business from a Cash-Eating Monster to a Money-Making Machine by Mike Michalowicz

The Artist's Way by Julia Cameron

$100M Offers: How to Make Offers So Good People Feel Stupid Saying No by Arjun Hormozi

Bird by Bird, by Anne Lamott

Bonus: Website Recomendations

Listing your art online provides you with a broader reach and access to a global audience. There are several online platforms where you can list your artwork. and here are a few of them. If you are wondering what platforms you can sell your artwork on, this chapter is the right one for you. Listed below are some of the most successful and well-known websites and platforms on which you can sell your artwork.

- Etsy: www.etsy.com
- Saatchi Art: www.saatchiart.com
- Art Station: www.artstation.com
- Devian Arrt: www.deviantart.com
- Redbubble: www.redbubble.com
- Society6: www.society6.com
- Artfinder: www.artfinder.com
- Fine Art America: www.fineartamerica.com
- Big Cartel: www.bigcartel.com
- Instagram: www.instagram.com
- Facebook Marketplace: www.facebook.com
- Art Pal: www.artpal.com
- Artsy: www.artsy.net
- Houzz: www.houzz.in

Acknowledgements

THANK YOU! To my life experiences, my gurus I got in the form of books, my parents, who gave me the support they could,

Utkarsh, my brother, for sometimes believing in me and being my best critic,

My professors at MSU built my base in architecture, especially Mayur Gupta, for his guidance and love.

To my team, especially Lachenba, who believed in me when I had zero money to start my business, and to Keyur, who gave me 20k when I had no one to help me kickstart.

My mentors Avi Arya, Puja Puneet, Gopal Krishnan, and a bunch of others have stolen from me to help me make this business my own.

To all my students who trusted me and made FAT World School.

Archana Kamal, my talented student, for listening patiently and helping me get this book done.

And the biggest thank you to all the failures, heartbreaks, challenges, and bad experiences that made me stronger inside out.

And last but not least

THANKS TO ME FOR WHO I AM.

Thank you, thank you, thank you :)

Want to consult for your dream art business??

Connect with Rashmi Suthar!

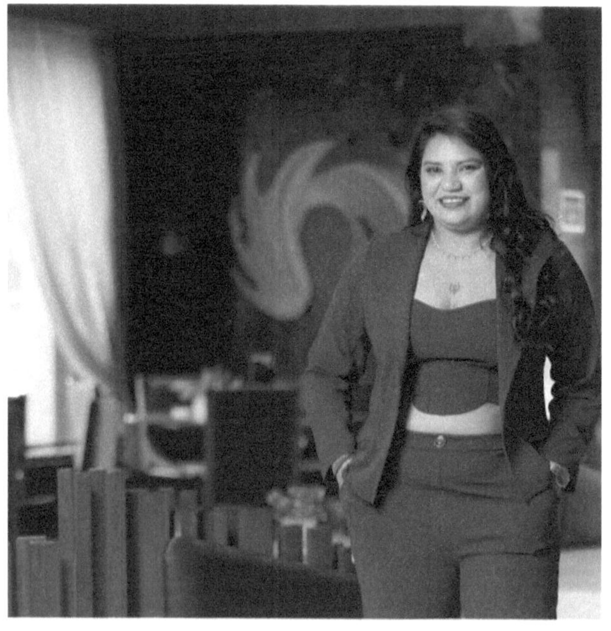

Want to book a call with us? Get in touch.

@artbizguru_official
www.artbizguru.com
9353860759
fatventures10@gmail.com

Afterword

Now that I am an art business coach, moving towards a more aligned purpose with business in life, I would like to summarize and tell you that you need to first feel aligned with your energy and purpose in life.

Find out how to start your business and take action fast. learn to design the product well, learn the sales, marketing and branding, all of this that we have discussed in the book hopefully will help you as an artist to kick start your career and

I hope that, as you are reading this last page, you feel more equipped with the necessary mindset and knowledge that you need to start and run your art business. Thank you for coming this far. Have a lovely time creating beautiful art and here is wishing you all the best for a successful and fulfilling art career.

Also, Congratulations now you are a SMARTPRENEUR! It is time to implement it all. Do join our free webinar, and get in touch with us to meet a beautiful community of like-minded artists here at FAT World School. We are waiting for you at this end. Scan the code and get more resources.
Take Care,
Rashmi.